ICNC **MONOGRAPH** SERIES

Prison Hunger Strikes in Palestine

A Strategic Perspective

Malaka Mohammed Shwaikh and Rebecca Ruth Gould

ICNC
PRESS

Contents

EXECUTIVE SUMMARY

This monograph reveals in unprecedented detail how prison hunger strikes achieve monumental feats of resistance through the weaponization of lives. It shows that sometimes the need for dignity (*karamah*) and freedom (*hurriya*) trump hunger and thirst.

The research fully centers the voices of hunger strikers to better understand their strategic choices, communication and coordination tactics, and negotiation process. Transnational in its approach, it also relies on extensive interviews with Palestinian, South African, Kurdish, Irish, and British former prisoners and hunger strikers.

The study is analytical in its framing, exploring the different forms and tactics of hunger strikes in a carceral space designed to cut prisoners off from the rest of the world. The analysis results in multiple lessons and actionable takeaways that will be as useful to prison activists as they will be to their allies around the world. These include:

Lessons for the Public:

- Hunger strikers prepare themselves to give their lives for the ethical goal of preserving their dignity.

- Even when they embark on a strike while in solitary confinement, hunger strikers never act alone.

Takeaways for Sympathizers and Allies:

- Solidarity organizations and individuals can use a wide range of solidarity actions to raise the visibility of prison hunger strikes for the wider public.

- Engagement with media is crucial, as it can increase public support for hunger strikers and raise the visibility of solidarity actions.

Takeaways for Hunger Strikers:

- Direct the narrative away from self-harm: death is never a desired result. Nor is death— or any kind of self-harm—the ultimate purpose.

- Pace the strikes to maximize mobilization: Frequency is an important factor when choosing to embark on a strike. An extended pause between hunger strikes along with different strategic planning may cause public support for the prisoners to swell.

- Hold awareness sessions: Awareness-raising sessions among prisoners are needed to answer difficult questions about whether hunger strikes are needed and whether they can bring about the desired outcomes in the particular circumstances of the prisoners.

- Minimize the risks: it is crucial for a prison hunger striker to minimize the danger the strike poses to themselves and their fellow prisoners, without compromising the effectiveness of their strike. This can be achieved through holding awareness sessions to discuss lessons from previous hunger strikes and issues that may have increased or decreased their effectiveness.

Glossary of Abbreviations

ANC	**African National Convention**
CHRI	Center for Human Rights in Iran
ICSFT	**International Council Supporting Fair Trial and Human Rights**
IPS	Israeli Prison Services
IRA	**Irish Republican Army**
OPT	Occupied Palestinian Territories
PA	**Palestinian Authority**
PFLP	Popular Front for the Liberation of Palestine
PHRI	**Physicians for Human Rights–Israel's**
PLO	Palestinian Liberation Organization
PPSMO	**Palestinian Prisoners Society**
WMA	World Medical Association

INTRODUCTION:
HUNGER STRIKES
AND PRISON RESISTANCE

In 2015, Palestinian baker Khader Adnan was imprisoned in an Israeli jail under "administrative detention," without charge or trial. Due to his lengthy hunger strike, Adnan was at the point of starvation. Bedridden, hospitalized, and in critical condition on the 55th day of his strike, his wife, Randa Mousa, and their six children were allowed to visit him. Their 45-minute visit turned into a long vigil of solidarity led by family members on the hospital's sidewalk, demanding Adnan's immediate release. The supportive community in which they lived could not accept the sight of a woman and her children sleeping alone and away from their home. Prison solidarity activists circulated calls for action over social media asking for volunteers to join a sit-in. Within a short time, additional supporters arrived, increasing the pressure on the Israeli authorities to release Mousa's husband. Hundreds of Palestinians camped outside the Israeli hospital where Adnan was imprisoned. Beneath Adnan's window, supporters chanted "*thawritna thawrit insan, qa'dha Khader Adnan*"—"Our revolution is a human revolution, declared by Khader Adnan." Adnan heard the chants and asked the Israeli authorities to suspend negotiations for a few minutes. Soon, his hunger strike paid off. The sit-in outside his window put pressure on the authorities to conclude negotiations with Adnan and meet his demand for freedom. He ended his hunger strike and was released on December 23, 2015.

While Adnan's case is a striking example of a successful hunger strike supported by a sit-in, it is not unique. Around the world, and with increasing frequency since the 1960s, imprisoned political activists have refrained from eating as a means of resisting the power of the carceral state. Hunger strikes are not a new or uniquely modern practice. Starvation as a form of protest dates to the beginning of recorded history and is well documented in medieval Ireland in particular (Fierke 2012, 108). This practice is also deeply rooted in Irish social justice politics (Beresford 1987, 7). As *cealachan* ("achieving justice by starvation") or *troscadh* ("fasting on or against a person"), hunger strikes were part of the *Senchus Mor* (the "Great Ancient Tradition"), a civil code that was one of the most significant legal texts of early Ireland (Ellmann 1993, 12–13; Beresford 1987, 14). This legal text specified the circumstances under which hunger strikes could be used to "recover a debt, or right a perceived injustice, [for] the complainant fasting on the doorstep of the defendant" (Beresford 1987, 14; Hughes 2017, 25). When someone committed an injustice, the wronged person would fast on the doorstep of the wrongdoer. If they were allowed to die while fasting, the wrongdoer would be held responsible for the death and would have to pay compensation to the family. In the words of former Irish hunger striker, Pat Sheehan, who embarked on the 1981 hunger strike in Northern Ireland:

In the past, if someone committed an injustice on you, you should go to their doorstep and fast on their doorstep until that injustice has been eroded. And that was the mindset we had in terms of going on hunger strike. We were not going on hunger strike to die. We were going on hunger strike to show the world that an injustice had been done on us. (Mashharawi 2014)

This practice exerted a moral force in Ireland because of the honor attached to hospitality and the dishonor attached to a person starving outside one's home (Scanlan, Stoll, and Lumm 2008, 314).

As time passed, more hunger strikes were documented. Ireland continued to lead the way. One of the most significant hunger strikes in Northern Ireland was the 1981 strike that not only raised awareness of the plight of the Irish Republican Army (IRA) prisoners but changed the overall struggle in the country. Ten Irish men died while on the strike, including strike leader Bobby Sands, who had just won the parliamentary elections. Having become the youngest member of the UK Parliament at the time, Sands was unable to take his seat in the Commons due to his incarceration.

The tradition of hunger strikes as a form of resistance is not unique to Ireland and was also an established practice by others elsewhere. In British India (1858–1947), the practice of "sitting dharna" or "sitting down to die by hunger strike" was abolished by a government decree in 1861 (Beresford 1987, 15; Knight 2012, 1–162). However, this decree did not stop it from being used as a method of coercion against authority into the mid-twentieth century. It was often employed by peasants fasting at moneylenders' doors, aiming to gain more time to repay their debts (Beresford 1987, 15–16), similar to the practice proscribed in the *Senchus Mor* of Ireland. Likewise, in 1909, the British suffragettes embarked on hunger strikes to demand the vote for women (Crawford 2003, 306; Purvis 2009). Later, in 1972, Cesar Chavez embarked on a hunger strike to demand farm workers' rights in the United States (Farraj 2016; Kallen 2010, 124). More recently, prisoners in the Guantanamo Bay Detention Camp in Cuba have embarked on several hunger strikes. The first of these ended in 2005 as prison authorities agreed to provide prisoners with better access to books and bottled drinking water (Gillan 2005; Simanowitz 2015; Farraj 2016; Begg interview).

This monograph sees hunger strikes as a practice in which prisoners' lives are weaponized through starvation to achieve political goals, from demanding better imprisonment conditions to freedom. The study is particularly concerned with the link between hunger strikes and political mobilization in the modern period. We analyze a series of collective and individual hunger strikes from 1968 to 2018, with a particular focus on the Palestinian context of colonization and apartheid. At times, we have brought other examples from other contexts, namely from South Africa, Iran, Turkey, Northern Ireland, and the US detention camp in Guantánamo

Bay. These examples offer a synoptic panorama of the many ways in which prisoners have resisted the state by refusing food and sometimes water. We are interested in the strategic means through which they have achieved their demands.

Although often viewed as powerless, incarcerated people have agency. At different times and places, they have found individual and collective ways to resist the underlying reasons for or conditions of their imprisonment. Resistance actions by prisoners include individual hunger strikes like that of Khader Adnan, general strikes, boycotts, and work stoppages. Prisoners have also refused communication with their jailers, using the required forms of address, performing prison headcount drills, and violating prison rules. Palestinian male prisoners have even smuggled their sperm to their wives back home for in vitro fertilization (IVF) treatment. Dallal al-Zabn was able to get pregnant in early 2012 using her husband's sperm—the first documented success—smuggled from the jail in a small plastic bag placed in a date (Touma 2021).

According to former Palestinian hunger striker Ayman al-Sharawna (2014), hunger strikes come as a last resort after other resistance methods to address grievances fail. In this context, al-Sharawna notes that a collective hunger strike in 2004 was launched after "the Israeli prison service started to withdraw our privileges."

> *So, we began protesting by rejecting meals and refusing to go out into the prison yard. Then we stopped clinic and court visits but none of it changed anything. So, we decided to start a mass hunger strike. The Israeli prison service interpreted our move as declaration of a war and launched harsher measures against us.* (Mashharawi 2014)

Furthermore, prisoners tried to obtain contraband items such as mobile phones (Shwaikh 2018; Al-Faleet and Abu Atwan interviews). They also tried prison breaks, most recently on September 6, 2021, when six Palestinian prisoners successfully escaped Jalbou Israeli Prison through a tunnel they dug (Shwaikh 2021). There are very few successful prison breaks in Palestinian history. The best known was in 1987 when six prisoners cut iron bars and escaped Gaza Israeli Prison (Bab el-Wad 2017). Also, in 1996, three prisoners in Ashkelon Prison dug a tunnel, two of whom escaped disguised in women's clothing while the third was caught because of his men's shoes (Metras 2021). In prison breaks, prisoners use what scarce tools are available in the prison, from spoons to digging tunnels to Coca-Cola to melting iron-reinforced concrete in the ground—a process that may take several months, if not years, to plan and execute. These are just some of the resistance tactics used in prisons—places seen as the most restrictive for any independent action—and prove unarmed resistance is neither impossible nor futile.

Political prisoners have also engaged in protests. In January 2019, prisoners across three Israeli prisons protested an unannounced prison cell search, according to the Israeli

7

newspaper *Haaretz* (Breiner 2019a and 2019b).[1] In this case, 17 Palestinian prisoners and six Israeli guards were injured. Protesting from within the confines of a prison is a courageous act that involves high risk, yet this has not deterred political prisoners from resisting oppression using this tactic.

Together, hunger strikes, work stoppages, smuggling, noncompliance, boycotts, prison breaks, and protests comprise the broad repertoire of resistance tactics employed by Palestinian political prisoners in Israeli prisons. This monograph seeks to better understand the role, dynamics, and impact of hunger strikes waged by those who, from the outside, may appear to be completely powerless.

Research Focus

Prison Hunger Strikes in Palestine focuses in unprecedented detail on a specific form of resistance through the weaponization of lives: the prison hunger strike. Hunger strikes are typically framed as a form of nonviolent resistance. In the only extended study of hunger strikes as nonviolent resistance, Scanlan, Stoll, and Lumm recognize that "little is known as to how the body of existing hunger strikes may be understood collectively as a protest form" (2008, 277). The authors point out that scholarship has not yet attempted to "theorize hunger strikes from a comparative perspective that focuses on and starts with them as a protest form of their own, or that places hunger strikes in the larger theoretical literature on social movements and nonviolent action" (282). Taking up the challenge, they situate hunger strikes in the context of nonviolent action, a framework that we do not adopt in this monograph. Instead, this study conceptualizes hunger strikes as a form of political noncooperation and offers an in-depth strategic analysis of the dynamics of the hunger strike itself. We have merged the traditional conceptualization of hunger strikes as a resistance action with the strategic understanding of hunger strikes as the weaponization of life, used first by Banu Bargu (2014) in her research on Kurdish hunger strikers in Turkish prisons. Drawing from lengthy interviews, we offer first-hand accounts of this form of political mobilization carefully attenuated to the context of incarceration.[2] We offer practitioners and students of resistance a clear outline of the dynamics of hunger strikes and the lessons learned from such actions.

Scanlan, Stoll, and Lumm consider a hunger strike to be in effect when "an actor voluntarily refuses to consume the food or nourishment necessary to sustain life as a sociopolitical protest

---

1   Whereas Israeli media outlets receive exclusive access to news from Israeli prisons and Israeli prison staff, Palestinian media does not. Israeli prison authorities sometimes ban, and often restrict, families and lawyers from visiting Palestinian prisoners.

2   Unless otherwise noted, quotations in this study from hunger strikers and their family members are drawn from original interviews by the authors. Details of these interviews are provided in the Appendix.

tactic to achieve nonviolent change" (2008, 278). In his *Dictionary of Power and Struggle*, renowned nonviolent action theorist Gene Sharp defines a hunger strike similarly as the "refusal to eat with the aim of forcing the opponents to grant demands but without serious efforts" to convert the official powerholders to the striker's cause (2012, 151). Sharp contrasts the hunger strike with the *satyagrahic* fast associated with Gandhi, which aims at converting the opponent to the striker's viewpoint. Character, intentions, and motives matter for the *satyagrahi,* whose goal is to melt the heart of the oppressor through self-starvation (Borman 1986). According to Sharp, a hunger strike is a strategic instrument of resistance that is not aimed at converting the opponent.

Sharp's focus on the transfer of power from those who hold it to those who resist applies to most prison hunger strikes. For example, hunger strikers take control over their own bodies in a context that gives complete control to prison authorities. Sharp notes that hunger strikes are "resorted to by prisoners whose other means of resistance are limited" (151). However, he provides minimal insight into the dynamics of the prison hunger strike. While we follow Sharp's definition of the hunger strike, we also take up the unaddressed challenge of exploring its dynamics outside a nonviolent framework to establish what makes this method effective.

Hunger strikes have also been framed as civil resistance, a mode of political existence that we define as collective action outside the state's formal institutions that, in the words of Atack, "avoids the systematic or deliberate use of violence or armed force to achieve its political or social objectives" (2012, 202). While hunger strikes have long been considered a method of civil resistance, there has been relatively little research focused on this particular tactic. And while much work has been done on hunger strikes as a mode of civil resistance in other geographies—including Northern Ireland and Turkey—the study of Palestinian hunger strikes is still in its infancy. This is in contrast to other single civil resistance methods such as civil disobedience and boycotts—and other geographies such as South Africa and the United States—that have received greater attention among strategists and scholars of civil resistance (see Thoreau 1866; Arendt 1972; Habermas 1985). We argue that, when it comes to resisting oppression, hunger strikes matter as much as other civil resistance methods. Increasingly, hunger strikes have become the most effective means of bringing about political change within prisons compared to other means, including noncompliance.

Their need for dignity and freedom is so pressing that it can sometimes transcend or sublimate the feeling of hunger.

Not only have civil resistance scholars paid relatively scant attention to the method of a hunger strike; they have generally ignored the carceral context in which most hunger strikes occur. However, that context is extremely important given that no less than 69.9% of all 1,441 hunger strikes spanning the decades from 1904 to 2004 occurred within prisons (Scanlan, et

9

al. 2008, 297). Furthermore, 42.8% of the demands behind these hunger strikes centered on prison conditions and the justice system (295). This shows that the context of incarceration is not incidental to the dynamics of the hunger strike.

Careful examination of hunger strikes in prisons will enable the reader to better appreciate how political prisoners have created the conditions for their liberation. We focus on hunger strikes by people imprisoned as a result of their politically motivated actions—including political activism—and analyze them as a political resistance tactic that relies on the weaponization of lives. This monograph explores how political dynamics specific to incarceration shape this form of political noncooperation, often inspiring hunger strikes outside the context of incarceration.

Our research explores how political prisoners who embarked on hunger strikes—such as Khader Adnan, Samer Issawi, and Hana Shalabi—have a formidable weapon at their disposal: their bodies. They make history through self-discipline, self-sacrifice, and by 'weaponizing' life through the use of the body to embark on hunger strikes. While jailed for violating the legal norms of unjust regimes, prisoners turn their bodies into instruments of their political will by individually or collectively subordinating their need for food to their equally powerful need for dignity and freedom. Their need for dignity and freedom is so pressing that it can sometimes transcend or sublimate the feeling of hunger.

The following questions structure our discussion around hunger strikes in Palestinian contexts:

The Process of Hunger Striking

- How can seemingly powerless prisoners who lack freedom and resources plan for, launch, execute, and complete a hunger strike? (Chapter 3)

- How do prisoners communicate and coordinate their actions and decide on their demands? (Chapter 3)

- How do hunger strikers mobilize outside sympathizers, and what communication strategies do they use to reach allies outside prisons? (Chapter 3)

The Roles of Hunger Strikers

- What role does each prisoner play in the execution of the hunger strike? (Chapters 1, 2, and 3)

- What is the role of leadership, unity, and discipline in the prison hunger strike? (Chapters 1 and 3)

- What are the gendered implications of hunger strikes? (Chapter 2)

Repression

- What repressive measures do the authorities use against hunger strikers? (Chapter 4)

- How do prisoners try to ensure that repression by the prison authorities will backfire and increase sympathy for the strikers? (Chapter 4)

- How are Israeli means of repression gendered? (Chapter 4)

The Negotiation Process

- Under what circumstances do hunger strikers reach out to their jailers to win over their favors or even sympathy, and how is this helpful for the prisoners? (Chapter 5)

- How do hunger strikers leverage their strike actions when negotiating with their jailers? (Chapter 5)

- How and when do hunger strikers end their strike? (Chapter 5)

Success and Impacts of Hunger Striking

- What is needed for a successful hunger strike? (Chapter 6)

- What strategic factors related to the dynamics of hunger strikes shape their success or failure? (Chapter 6)

- Should hunger strikes that do not achieve any of their demands be understood as failed strikes? Is success to be measured only by the demands achieved? (Chapter 6)

By the end of the monograph, the reader will have a clear sense of how we have navigated these questions.

Background to the Israeli Imprisonment of Palestinians

Prisons are violent tools of the Israeli colonial project. Israel has used them since its creation in 1948 to incarcerate Palestinians and criminalize their resistance. Alongside the 4,650 Palestinian political prisoners in Israeli jails documented by the Palestinian human rights organization Addameer (2022), there are Palestinian political prisoners in Palestinian Authority and Hamas-run prisons (HRW 2016) that are not the focus of this research. This monograph focuses on Israeli jails. Table 1 lists their names (in English, Arabic, and Hebrew), locations, opening dates, and further details.

Table 1: Israeli Prisons

PRISON NAME	ARABIC AND HEBREW NAMES	LOCATION	OPENING DATE AND DETAILS
ISRAELI PRISONS IN 1948 PALESTINIAN AREAS (TERRITORIES CURRENTLY WITHIN ISRAEL)			
Ramleh Prison	سجن الرملة כלא רמלה	Located on the road separating the cities of Lod and Ramleh, north of Palestine	The establishment of this prison dates back to 1934, when the Soleil Bonnet Company built it for the benefit of the British Mandate as a *saraya* (a house where they receive official delegates). In 1948, it was seized by the Israeli army, which turned it into a control center. In 1953, the Israeli Military Intelligence (Aman) turned it into an investigation and arrest center for resistance fighters. Ramleh Prison currently serves as a transit site. Prisoners are relocated there from one prison before being transferred to another. It is a prison compound comprised of the following prison structures: (1) Ramleh Prison Hospital for treating prisoners, although prisoners interviewed for this work emphasize the lack of basic and necessary medical equipment; (2) Ayalon Prison; (3) Neve Tirza; and (4) Nitzan Prison.
Damoun Prison	سجن الدامون כלא דמון	Located among the bushes of Mount Carmel and on the road between Haifa and Atlit	Damoun Prison began to be constructed during the British Mandate due to the importance of the site on the coastal road that leads to the north of Palestine. It was established as a factory for smoke and tobacco, so it was built in a place where there is moisture to keep the smoke leaves. Damoun prisoners complain of the prevalence of severe humidity in the prison.
Shatta Prison	سجن شطة כלא שאטה	Located in the Jordan Valley, next to the Palestinian town of Baysan, south of the Sea of Galilee	The establishment of this prison dates back to the Khan Castle, which was built by the Ottomans, and then used by the British army. In 1953, Israel converted it into a prison.
Neve Tirza or Neve Tirtza	سجن نفي ترتسا כלא גלות תרצה	Located between the cities of Lod and Ramleh and near Ayalon Prison	Established in 1968, Neve Tirza is designated for Palestinian women prisoners and Israeli "criminal prisoners." It is part of the Ramleh Prison compound.
Kfar Yona	سجن كفار يونا בית סוהר כפר יונה	5 km west of the Palestinian city of Tulkarm in the West Bank	During the British Mandate, Kfar Yona was called Tigron Castle. It was captured by Israeli forces in the last months before the Arab armies entered Palestine in 1948 and the Iraqi forces subsequently took control of it. Abdul Karim Qassem established the headquarters for his leadership here. He handed over the place to the Jordanian army that left it when they withdrew. Israel opened it as a prison in 1968.

Table 1, cont'd

PRISON NAME	ARABIC AND HEBREW NAMES	LOCATION	OPENING DATE AND DETAILS
Ashkelon (Askalan) Prison	سجن عسقلان כלא אשקלון	Located in Ashkelon city, south of Palestine	This building was constructed during the British Mandate over Palestine as the headquarters for the British army command in the region, and it was used to receive official British delegations. It was officially opened as a prison on 11 February 1969. According to Addameer Prisoner Support and Human Rights Association (n.d., a), when the prison first opened, the prison guards forced prisoners "to pass in between two lines from the prison gates to the prison cells and rooms while beating them with batons all over their bodies." Addameer notes the prison has five sections, one of which is an isolation section. Another is the "shame" section, to the northwest of the prison, which houses prisoners who collaborated with the prison administration and the Shin Bin security services. There is also a wing for the Israeli Shabak (security services) where interrogation of Arab and Palestinian prisoners takes place.
Beersheba (Beer al-Saba') Prison	سجن بئر السبع כלא באר שבע	Located on the road between the cities of Beersheba and Eilat, south of Palestine	The Beersheba Prison complex consists of four prisons, each segregated from one another: Ohli Kedar and Eshel are for "security prisoners," Dekel is for "critical prisoners," and Ayla was established to become the first private prison but was then shut following a decision from the Supreme Court. The decision to establish it dates back to the 1968 discussions in the Israeli Knesset about prisons. It was completed and opened with the first batch of prisoners on 3 January 1970. The complex is used to isolate prisoners in specific cases like hunger strikes.
Nafha Prison	سجن نفحة כלא נפחא	The Negev desert in southern Palestine, 200 km south of Jerusalem	According to Addameer, the prison was used especially for "security prisoners" since opening 1 May 1980. It is considered one of the "most harsh and severe of the occupation prisons," and was renovated mainly to imprison leaders in the Palestinian prisoners' movement and isolate them from the rest of the prisoners' community (n.d., b). The desert prison is extremely cold during the winter and extremely hot during the summer.

13

PRISON NAME	ARABIC AND HEBREW NAMES	LOCATION	OPENING DATE AND DETAILS
ISRAELI PRISONS IN 1967 PALESTINIAN AREAS (OCCUPIED PALESTINIAN TERRITORIES)			
Hebron (Khalil) Prison	سجن الخليل כלא חברון	Located in the center of Hebron	The prison was built during the British Mandate of Palestine on the top of a hill. The Jordanian army used the building as a barracks for its army. In 1967, Israelis turned in it a police station, but they soon began to use it for all security service operations in and around the Hebron area.
al-Maskobiyya Prison (Russian Compound)	سجن المسكوبية (ساحة الروس) כלא מגרש הרוסים	Located on the western side of Jerusalem, next to the Israeli intelligence headquarters in al-Maskobiyya, or al-Rus [Russian], Square	Built during the British Mandate period as a police station to detain prisoners awaiting trial.
Ramallah Prison	سجن رام الله כלא רמאללה	Located in the north of Ramallah, in the West Bank	Built in the years of the British Mandate and used by the Jordanian army. Israel controlled it and used it as a headquarters for its security services in Ramallah and its surroundings.
Gaza (Central) Prison	سجن غزة المركزي (السرايا) הכלא המרכזי בעזה (אל-סראיה)	Located in the Rimal neighborhood in the center of Gaza City	Built during the British Mandate era. Gaza prison used to be the largest Israeli military site in the Gaza Strip. It houses the leadership of the Israeli army forces in the Gaza Strip, in addition to the offices of the Israeli intelligence service. It consisted of five sections for prisoners. After Israel occupied the Gaza Strip in 1967, Gaza Central Prison became known for its harsh conditions, as well as two escape attempts, namely: • Eight prisoners attempting to escape in 1983 with tools that were concealed. They were able to open the doors, but the prison administration discovered it before the prisoners left the prison wall. • The successful escape of six Islamic Jihad activists who managed to flee through a window on 17 May 1987.

Addameer Prisoner Support and Human Rights Association registers annually at least 700 cases of the prosecution—following arrest, interrogation, and detention—of Palestinian children from the Occupied West Bank in Israeli prisons and jails. The most common charge levied against them is stone throwing, a crime punishable under military law by up to 20 years in prison.

As of June 2022, there were a total of 170 Palestinian child prisoners in Israeli prisons. While the UN Convention on the Rights of the Child defines a child as anyone below age 18,

Israeli Military Order 132 classifies as an adult any Palestinian child between the ages of 16 and 18 who has been tried and sentenced more than once by the Israeli military courts. In sharp contrast, Israeli juvenile legislation defines Israeli children as those aged 18 and younger. Meanwhile, Palestinian children's sentences are determined based on their age when sentenced, not at the time when the "alleged offence was committed" (Addameer 2017b). There have been several cases of children accused of committing an offense when they were under the age of 16 who were punished as adults because they turned 16 while awaiting their sentencing. Since 2000, at least 12,000 Palestinian children have been detained (Addameer 2017a). These children experience all forms of harassment and torture: physical, psychological, and sexual. As one child reported, "More than one interrogator threatened to rape me, saying, 'If you do not want to talk from your mouth we will make you talk from elsewhere.'" The child

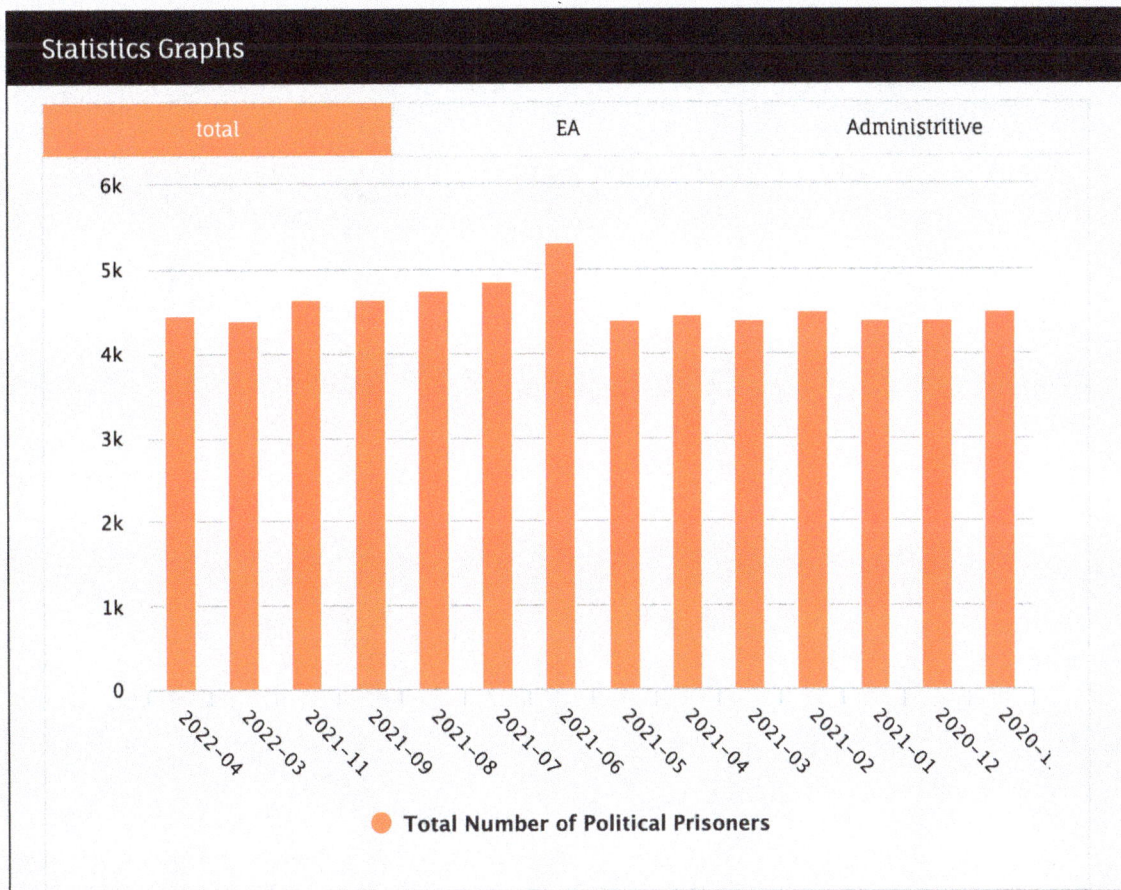

FIGURE 1: NUMBER OF PALESTINIAN POLITICAL PRISONERS IN ISRAELI PRISONS

(November 2020–April 2022. Addameer Graph.
Note that the passage of time in this graph is conveyed right-to-left)

added, "I felt very scared and confessed to something that I did not do and that never happened" (Addameer 2017a, 10).

Over the past 50 years, approximately 10,000 Palestinian women have been arrested or detained under Israeli military orders. Like all prisoners, women are exposed to torture and violence, including psychological torture and abusive treatment throughout the process of their arrest and detention, sexual violence, beatings, insults, threats, body searches, and sexually explicit harassment (Addameer 2017a). Addameer shows that 32 Palestinian female prisoners were in Israeli prisons in June 2022. In the same month, there were 130 political prisoners from the 1948 territories (Israel), 450 from east Jerusalem, 200 from the Gaza Strip, and 7 Palestinian Legislative Council members. In terms of duration of detention, 499 prisoners were serving a sentence above 20 years and 551 prisoners were serving life sentences. 214 were already serving more than 20 years, and 37 prisoners were serving more than 25 years. 25 prisoners have been in Israeli jails since before Oslo Accords were signed in 1993. These numbers remain constant. When they change, they generally increase, as Figure 1 demonstrates.

Outside Israeli prisons, Palestinians are subjected to constant violence at the hands of Israeli colonial forces. Such tensions have a long history. When the League of Nations placed Palestine under the British Mandate in 1922, tensions arose between the Palestinians and the Jewish immigrants. This came to a head in 1948, when the British departed and the foundation of the State of Israel was proclaimed. That year was marked by what several historians have described as the ethnic cleansing of Palestinians. This event involved the destruction of Palestinian homes and is referred to by Palestinians as the *Nakba* (Arabic for "catastrophe") (Pappé 2006a; Pappé 2006b, 6–20; Al-Rimmawi and Zaidan 2013, 216, 222). Palestinians who were expelled by military force became either internally displaced persons or refugees.

Further military conflicts have occurred since 1948, including but not limited to the 1967 Six-Day War between Israel and several Arab countries, following which Israel occupied the rest of Palestine and neighboring Arab regions, including Syria's Golan Heights and Egypt's Sinai Peninsula. Later, Palestinian resistance intensified with uprisings, including the First Intifada (Arabic for "uprising") beginning in 1987 and, in 2000, the Second Intifada.

There is a longstanding debate about whether these areas are occupied or colonized (Veracini 2013). In our view, occupation is one phase of colonization, and the occupation has turned into long-term colonization. Israel is a settler-colonial state that has violated the rules of occupation, as outlined in international law. We also recognize that the term "Occupied Palestinian Territories" (OPT) denoting the areas seized in 1967 fails to convey that the areas seized earlier by Israel in 1948 were also part of Palestine. Where context dictates, we use the phrase "historical Palestine" to describe the pre-1948 Palestinian areas. "Occupation" and "colonization" are sometimes used interchangeably.

Following the Second Intifada in 2000, Israel began to increase its reliance on administrative detention as a form of collective punishment in which the Israeli military court system allows for the indefinite detention of Palestinians with no charge (see Figure 2). As of November 2021, 500 of the 4,650 Palestinian political prisoners are under administrative detention. They are denied the right to stand trial, and the evidentiary basis (if any) for the charges against them is not disclosed to the prisoners or their lawyers (Baker and Matar 2011; Addameer 2017b; Pelleg-Sryck 2011, 123–134; Sarahna and Qadmani interviews).

B'Tselem, the Israeli Information Center for Human Rights in the Occupied Territories (founded in 1989), describes administrative detention in its reports as "incarceration without trial or charge, alleging that a person plans to commit a future offense." Administrative detention has "no time limit, and the evidence on which it is based is not disclosed" (2017). Israel

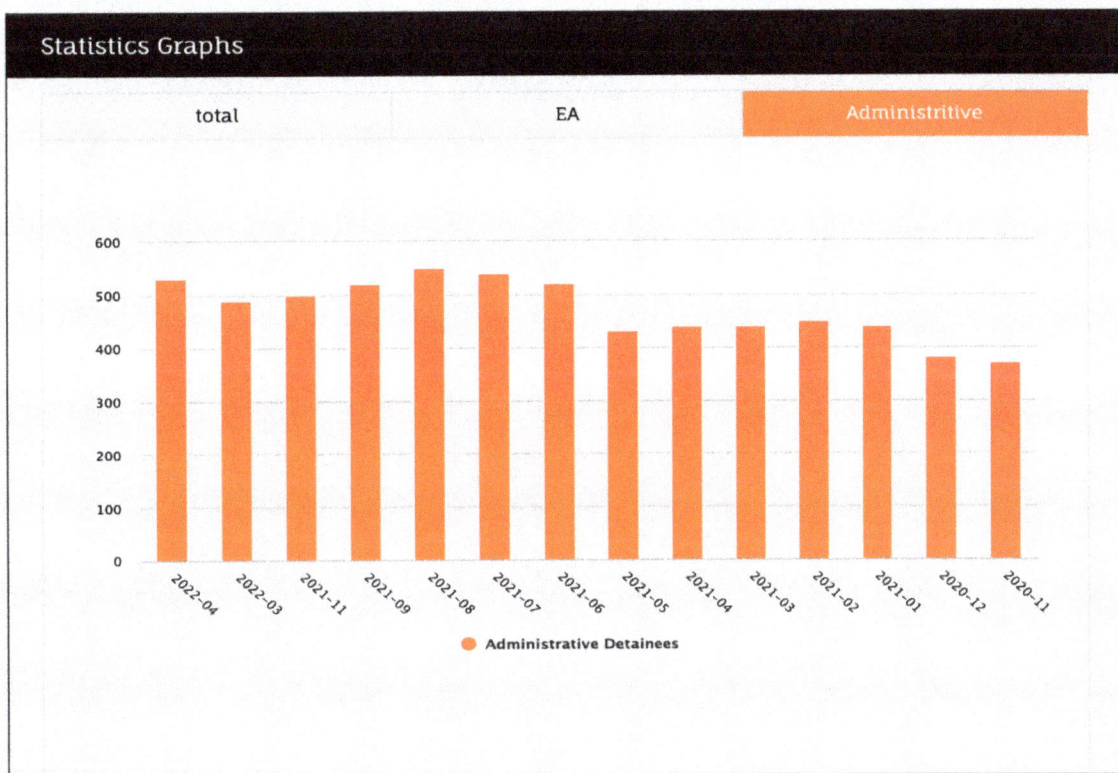

FIGURE 2: NUMBER OF PALESTINIAN ADMINISTRATIVE DETAINEES IN ISRAELI PRISONS

(November 2020–April 2022. Addameer Graph. Note that the passage of time moves right-to-left.)

17

employs this measure "extensively and routinely, and has used it to hold thousands of Palestinians for lengthy periods of time." And while Israeli prison authorities claim that all detention orders are formally reviewed, this is "merely a semblance of judicial oversight, as detainees cannot reasonably mount a defence against undisclosed allegations" (2017). International law clearly rejects such arbitrariness in detention. One example is from Article 9(1) of the International Covenant on Civil and Political Rights (ICCPR 1996), which reads: "Everyone has the right to liberty and security of person. No one shall be subjected to arbitrary arrest or detention. No one shall be deprived of his liberty except on such grounds and in accordance with such procedure as are established by law."

Since 2007, Palestinians in the Gaza Strip have lived under a military blockade that makes it nearly impossible for them to travel freely. In the West Bank, regular Israeli military raids of homes in the middle of the night often lead to more arrests. The two million Palestinians who live in Israel are treated as second-class citizens and are subject to persistent discrimination from Israeli laws and policies (Adalah 2019). Freedom of speech and freedom of movement are radically curtailed for Palestinians by unjust laws and policies. In the Occupied West Bank alone, more than 7,000 permanent road obstacles control Palestinian movement (UN OCHA 2018).

Palestinians in Israeli prisons suffer—and die—from torture and poor living conditions. Since 1967, the Palestinian Prisoners Society (PPSMO) has documented 72 deaths due to torture (Abu Samra 2020). Prisoners who suffer from dangerous ailments are usually released when their health condition reaches an irreversible stage, but they are then refused permission to travel abroad to seek treatment (Addameer 2013, pp. 23, 105, 112). One early account of the conditions in Israeli prisons came in 1975 from Israeli journalist Sylvia Adiv (1978), who wrote of the prisons:

> *Subhuman... terribly overcrowded; the cells are dark and damp.... Food is meager both in quality and quantity.... The sanitary conditions are miserable.... Medical care is given to the prisoner only when his condition is critical. The assumption which underlies the policy of the Prison Service is that a denial of liberty is not enough; the prisoner should be oppressed by every possible means. The slogan is: "A good prisoner is a broken prisoner."*

Another account by former Palestinian political prisoner Issam Abdel-Hadi (Antonius 1980, 40) describes the torture of female prisoners:

> *I used to see girls returning, beaten, from an interrogation. Ne'met Kamal ... came out gasping and choking, her hand broken and flapping at the wrist; I did not think she would*

live through the night. It was a common sight to see girls being carried back to their cells because they could not walk.

It is within this historical context and these chilling prison conditions that Palestinian political prisoners have embarked on hunger strikes for the past half-century to resist the oppression of the Israeli settler-colonial system.

Roadmap

Chapter 1 discusses this study's approach and methodology and clarifies its key concepts, addressing questions central to our framing of prisons as spaces of power and resistance, with hunger strikes as the ultimate means of prison resistance. Chapter 2 examines different types of hunger strikes—collective and individual—and explains the demands of collective hunger strikes. We then closely examine six hunger strikes, presenting the cases of Awni al-Sheikh, Etaf Ilian, Mona Qa'dan, Hana Shalabi, Shireen Issawi, and Samer Issawi. Coming from diverse socio-economic backgrounds, ages, and locations, each of them embarked on individual hunger strikes in Israeli prisons. They represent a wide range of political affiliations, including members of the Palestinian political parties Fatah, Hamas, Islamic Jihad, and the Popular Front for the Liberation of Palestine (PFLP).

Chapter 3 examines the process through which prison hunger strikes develop in the Palestinian context. This discussion includes pre-strike planning and coordination, the importance of having a unified prisoners' movement, as well as a unified and organized leadership, communication strategies, and, finally, prisoners' letters to the outside world.

Chapter 4 considers efforts on the part of prison authorities to repress strike organizing, activists' tactics for securing domestic and international sympathy, and strikers' strategies to escalate and de-escalate their prison resistance—including pushing for, entering into, and leading negotiations with prison authorities. The repression methods examined are force-feeding and banishing prisoners to remote areas (here exemplified by Palestine and Lebanon's Ansar prisons). The chapter concludes by considering how hunger strikers respond to repression. Chapter 5 more closely examines the process by which hunger strikers negotiate their demands with the prison authorities.

With the first five chapters concluded, our synoptic framework yields to more detailed case studies. Chapter 6 addresses the efficacy of hunger strikes, grouping outcomes in ways that help to measure their success and failure and to assess their domestic and international impact. Outcomes that follow from prison hunger strikes include gaining the right to family visits, access to lawyers, essential resources, and education, as well as an end to—or pause in—solitary confinement, administrative detention, and separation from other prisoners.

Chapter 7 offers takeaways for prisoners engaged in hunger strikes, their supporters and potential international allies, researchers, civil society groups on the frontlines of these struggles, the general public, and, finally, civil resisters directly engaged in these campaigns. We also extract lessons from the cases and dynamics introduced and ask what has enabled hunger strikes to succeed in the past, to formulate principles that will increase their chances for success in the future. Finally, we examine why prisoners embark on hunger strikes in the first place and how those outside the prison can support them. Solidarity, we argue, should be conceived as a verb, an action that challenges power imbalances and that pushes for justice on the ground.

Drawing from the proposed typology of the different kinds of prison hunger strikes, *Prison Hunger Strikes in Palestine* positions readers and activists to consider how the dynamics and outcomes of past prison hunger strikes can help to make future strikes more effective. For those engaged in hunger strikes, we distill lessons that may save their lives and protect their health.

Chapter 1. Hunger Strikes
in Theory and Practice

As a means of resisting injustice, the practice of starving for a cause long predates the modern era. Hunger striking can be traced back to antiquity (Russell 2005). In the past as well as in the present, hunger strikes have often been adopted as a last resort after all other means of addressing repression have failed. This chapter explains the methodology of this study and clarifies the key concepts that inform the modern deployment of hunger strikes. It also discusses the ambiguities of violence in the context of hunger striking and the "weaponization of life," by which we mean the use of one's life to advance objectives that, although personal, have political ramifications and consequences. Finally, this chapter briefly examines the immediate success and longer-term effects—or effectiveness—of prison hunger strikes.

Research Approach and Methodology

This study focuses primarily on Palestinians incarcerated by Israel who engage in hunger strikes while imprisoned. It also examines the strategic dynamics surrounding their hunger strikes. Alongside our primary focus on Palestinian prisoners, we also engage with primary and secondary sources concerning prison hunger strikes in other contexts, led largely by political prisoners in Northern Ireland and South Africa. The examples provided from these global contexts aim to contribute to a fuller understanding of the dynamics, processes, and impacts of hunger strikes for strikers and their allies.

Why is Palestine the overarching framework for this analysis? Palestine holds a particularly important position in the study of prison hunger strikes on grounds of historical continuity from as early as 1968—one year after the Israeli occupation of all of Palestine that followed the Six-Day War. Since then, hunger strikes have become a frequent and popular method for imprisoned Palestinians to resist their jailers and the settler-colonial policies that led to their imprisonment. They have also helped prisoners garner outside attention, sympathy, and solidarity. Furthermore, Palestinian hunger strikers have inspired other hunger strikes around the world, from Ireland to Algeria to South Africa.

Since 1968—the year with which this study begins—Palestine has been the site of many liberation struggles, including powerful resistance campaigns that have shaped the current thinking about civil resistance. Gene Sharp's ideas on civil resistance have also been relevant to Palestine and neighboring Middle Eastern countries, from the early stages of Iran's Islamic Revolution to Palestine's First Intifada to Egypt's Arab Spring (Khosrokhavar 2016, 283; Ziv

1989; Safieh 1987). Yet, many traditions of civil resistance in the Middle East predate the work of scholars like Sharp, including movements in nineteenth-century Algeria and Iran against foreign domination, in Egypt against the British (Rahal 2013; Abdalla and Arafa 2013; Keddie 2013; Sazegara and Stephan 2009), and in Palestine against the Ottomans, during the British Mandate, and, later, against Israel's occupation (Qumsiyeh 2011; King 2007). The prolonged encounters with state violence experienced by Middle Eastern revolutionaries and activists have led to diverse perspectives on resistance. Both armed struggle and civil resistance (which are not understood here as antonyms) have a long history in the Middle East. At times they have been used strategically, and at other times not, but they have set a precedent for other regions to resist occupation and colonization.

Our first-hand access to prison hunger strikers within Palestine (including the Gaza Strip, which has been under Israeli siege since 2007) has allowed for the development of a cutting-edge understanding of this under-researched phenomenon. In addition to its many ethnographic interviews (listed in the Appendix), this study is also informed by archival materials, news sources dating back to 1968, and social media posts by activists and their family members. This wide range of sources enables a comparative and systematic account of prison hunger strikes and their impact. In this way, this monograph develops several specific case studies across different times and locations in Palestine while extracting broader lessons.

A large volume of the data contained herein is original and unique to this project, and it has been subjected to systematic and comparative classification and analysis. Uncorroborated sources have been identified as such and critically interrogated. This research was undertaken to develop an exportable theoretical model that would help scholars and activists come to grips with the political function of prison hunger strikes, while advancing knowledge of political mobilization across a range of anti-colonial, decolonial, and neo-imperial[3] contexts.

Clarifying Key Concepts

Civil resistance scholarship recognizes that a frequent practitioner of political violence can engage in civil resistance in certain strategic circumstances. In light of this, hunger strikes are typically considered acts of civil resistance, regardless of the striker's general relationship to political violence in other circumstances. Following Schock (2003; 2005), this study of prison hunger strikes as a weaponization of lives acknowledges the literature that frames hunger strikes as a resistance tactic regardless of strikers' broader life trajectories or whether strikers proclaim a moral commitment or preference for nonviolence. We recognize that civil resistance

---

3   "Neo-imperial" for our purposes refers to the policy of extending a state's power and clout through hegemonic means including military, economic, cultural, and/or political pressure to control, force, and/or influence change on other countries.

methods are available to anyone, including insurgents and state actors who have also used violence. There are several documented examples when violent campaigns have embraced nonviolent actions for strategic and pragmatic reasons to achieve their political objectives (Dudouet 2015).

In other words, we are not concerned with defining the hunger strike as violent or nonviolent. We recognize that this binary can be dehumanizing for political prisoners embarking on resistance actions in Israeli prisons. Instead, we focus on the strategies and organizing methods behind hunger strikes, including those conducted by actors who are associated—whether by themselves or by others—with previously using violent tactics. Furthermore, prisoners' personal intentions and beliefs do not limit the scope of this investigation of hunger strike actions as acts of political mobilization or as part of the repertoire of strategic civil resistance.

But is Not Self-Harm Violent?

If civil resistance is a form of popular struggle that does not involve the direct threat or use of violence, how violence is defined affects the classification of hunger strikes as a civil resistance method. Many civil resistance researchers define violent tactics as actions that directly harm others (Chenoweth and Stephan 2011). Qumsiyeh writes that violence "consists of actions that harm others on the assumption that this will help achieve a concrete result or goal" (2012, 4). This study understands violence in its broadest physical and structural forms. Prisons are violent spaces that violate prisoners' basic rights. Prison hunger strikes, as resistance tactics, do not directly harm others. Rather, they are a response to the violence intrinsic to the carceral condition. This discussion moves away from binaries of violent–nonviolent and civil–armed resistance that may limit prisoners' agency.

Beyond self-immolation and hunger strikes, few other civil resistance tactics involve direct self-harm. Hunger strikes rely on willed starvation that harms the striker's body. To the extent that they inflict harm, prison hunger strikes are an assault on a certain condition or state of life: the strikers' imprisoned bodies. Were they to impose the same denial of food on another person, it would rightly be regarded as torture under international—and much domestic—law, and thus as a kind of violence.

In their struggle for individual and group rights, hunger strikers assert their dignity and agency. They do not undermine anyone's dignity. The infliction of self-harm and death are not to be counted among hunger strikers' goals. While death is a possibility, it is not a likely outcome. Only six percent of hunger strikes globally result in the striker's death in 1,441 hunger strikes reported between 1906 and 2004 (Scanlan, et al. 2008, 299). The primary goal of prison hunger strikes is not starvation but freedom or, at minimum, the altering of the circumstances of imprisonment.

In the words of Khader Adnan, whose 2005 hunger strike mobilized Palestinian society, "We do not strike because we want to die.... We sacrifice so much to live in dignity [*karama*]." Adnan's choice of the word *karama* resonates with human rights discourse that has enshrined the concept of dignity in the United Nations Universal Declaration of Human Rights. *Karama* resonates even more deeply in the Arabic context, wherein it functions alongside terms like "freedom" (*hurriya*) and "humanity" (*insaniyya*). Prisoners embark on hunger strikes to demand the collective right of an imprisoned people to be treated with *insaniyya* (Hosseinioun 2017, 63). Tellingly, Adnan referred to his hunger strike as a "battle for dignity [*ma'rakat al-karama*]." Adnan's emphasis on dignity reaches beyond his individual self. Particularly in settler-colonial and neo-imperial contexts, prison hunger strikes represent the collective struggle of an entire people for political freedom. They are grounded in dignity, both of the individual and the collective, and derive their legitimacy from the extent to which prisoners can link their struggle for dignity in jails with the struggle for political freedom waged outside the prison cell.

On the Weaponization of Life

In contrast to most civil resistance tactics of protest, noncooperation, and intervention that are part of Sharp's categories of nonviolent methods, hunger strikes involve the weaponization of life, the framework adopted for this monograph. Political theorist Banu Bargu (2011; 2015; 2017) views hunger strikes as nonviolent toward others yet violent toward the self, thus justifying her provocative description of hunger strikes as the "weaponization of life." We recognize the direct self-harm that hunger strikes can potentially inflict, and thus adopt Bargu's concept to distinguish between hunger strikes and other civil resistance tactics. While the weaponization of life and the proximity of death is central to Bargu's analysis, the interviews conducted for this research show that the goal of prison hunger strikes is not death itself but ultimate liberation—not necessarily a liberation in the literal sense of release from prison but in the political sense of regaining power over one's oppressive jailers. This power is manifested when prison authorities are compelled by hunger strikes to meet prisoners' basic demands, an outcome that was achieved by several hunger strikers discussed in this study.

Adopting this framework means going beyond the traditional binary of nonviolent–violent resistance and foregrounding the human body in the hunger striking process, including its use as a weaponized life to achieve prisoners' demands. This weaponization entails the use of prison hunger strikers' bodies to pursue political ends, sometimes at risk to their lives (Bargu 2011, 3). These potential risks are recounted by ex-Irish hunger striker, Pat Sheehan, who embarked on his strike in 1981. Sheehan (2014) recounts being told by a consultant in a Belfast hospital four days before he ended the hunger strike that "even if I ended my hunger strike there and then, there was a good chance I would not survive because my liver was beginning to shut down and there was a chance that there may have been [irreparable] damage done

24

to it." Such bodily risks may prove fatal. Yet, because hunger strikes are contingent on the productive value of the strikers' lives, Bargu considers them to be weaponizations of *life* rather than of the *body* (2014, 14, 297; 2015, 1–36).

In a context wherein life—and the will to sacrifice it—is the primary source of agency, the body becomes a battleground on which this struggle takes place. The body also becomes a stage, and its withering away is used to attract external support from those outside the prison cell. In other words, the 'stage' allows for an audience and hence attracts external support, while the 'battleground' is the site of the conflict. Hunger strikers infuse their bodies with political and philosophical content with a meaning that may lead to death. But is it thereby violent, when death may be a consequence but not a goal? For Bargu (2011), assessing hunger strikes through a violent–nonviolent binary inevitably privileges the viewpoints and actions of the state actors responsible for the prisoner's incarceration. The unstated assumption that an act can only be violent or nonviolent rather than both or neither emerges from a state-oriented liberal tradition that is out of touch with what Walter Benjamin called "the tradition of the oppressed" (Benjamin 1968, 257). Specifically for the case at hand, the violent–nonviolent binary is disconnected from the lived experience of occupation. Such binaries are ethically problematic when uncritically applied to Palestinians and other groups who are labeled violent (Gould 2016). In adopting an outside perspective, they ignore the agency of the striker, whose decision to strike is a quest for freedom that cannot be understood in terms of the violent–nonviolent binary. When the hunger striker is thus stripped of agency and their quest for freedom is mislabeled, even the force-feeding of prisoners can be made to seem nonviolent—and thus moral—notwithstanding that prisoners have died as a result of the damage that this practice has inflicted on their bodies (Miller 2016). Meanwhile, the steadfast resistance of prisoners engaged in hunger strikes is labeled violent and thereby dismissed as immoral.

In a context wherein life—and the will to sacrifice it—is the primary source of agency, the body becomes a battleground on which this struggle takes place.

Our framework combines the traditional conceptualization of hunger strikes as civil resistance with a strategic understanding of hunger strikes as a weaponization of life. Hunger strikers weaponize their lives pragmatically by instrumentalizing their bodies. Hunger strikers' openness to death shapes the measures they take and may determine the effectiveness of their sacrifice. Death here is only a possible outcome, not the goal. In an interview from 2014, Palestinian hunger striker Ayman al-Sharawna recalled: "I still cannot believe that I endured 261 days of hunger strike. Those days were like a blur. I was anticipating death every single moment. I actually felt I was dead when I refused to drink water." Hana Shalabi recollected her hunger strike in similar terms: "I was sure I would eventually die in jail. The Israeli authorities were stubborn and I stuck to my guns. My health was deteriorating badly. I was absolutely certain I was going to die there."

The experience of Irish hunger striker Pat Sheehan was similar to that of Shalabi and al-Sharawna. "When we went on hunger strike," Sheehan recalled, "it was always very clear that if you are going on hunger strike, you are going to die. And, you have to be prepared for that" (2014). He further comments that hunger strikers "are prepared to give their own lives. They are prepared to give up everything, never to see their families again, never to see their children growing up. And, that is... an enormous sacrifice for any human being to make." The cases of al-Sharawna, Shalabi, and Sheehan reveal how embarking on a hunger strike leads a person to confront death. Even though death is not the goal of a hunger strike, it must be contemplated by those who undertake the strike as a potential outcome if their demands are not taken seriously by the prison authorities.

"Political Prisoners" and "Common Criminals"

This monograph rejects any effort to posit absolute distinctions between political prisoners (seen as moral and sympathetic) and common criminals (seen as immoral and unsympathetic). Given the range of reasons for the imprisonment of Palestinians in Israeli-run prisons, many hunger strikers find themselves behind bars due to their resistance to an oppressive settler-colonial state rather than due to acts that would be criminalized under normal circumstances. This makes straightforward distinctions between political and nonpolitical prisoners untenable, given the fluid status of criminality in settler-colonial contexts and the shifting space for dissent across different legal contexts.

Whereas Israeli prison authorities separate Palestinian political prisoners (or 'security' prisoners, to use Israeli terminology) from other prisoners, this monograph aims to center the ways in which prisoners and hunger strikers see themselves as political prisoners who are in Israeli prisons for resistance-related activities. Among our interviewees are Palestinians who were imprisoned for engaging in resistance actions, for participating in more institutional forms of social advocacy, and for being sympathetic but not particularly active in such movements, and also those who became politicized and mobilized in prison. This monograph is inclusive of all prisoners engaging in hunger strikes and concentrates on the use and effects of this particular tactic rather than on the reasons for the prisoners' incarceration.

Nevertheless, a hunger striker's sentencing—along with the conditions in which they live—affects the types of demands they can make. For example, it is not realistic for a prisoner charged with manslaughter or homicide to embark on a hunger strike to demand release from prison. There has been no such documented case in the Palestinian prisoners' movement. Prisoners convicted of such offenses often embark on hunger strikes to demand improvement in prison conditions. Those who demand release from jail are often under administrative detention—without charge or a trial—or have not been sentenced to life in prison.

Negotiating for Political Imprisonment

Across our various case studies, incarcerated persons demand to be classified as political prisoners. Palestinian prisoners in Israeli prisons insist on framing their struggle as political and anti-colonial. Only this paradigm considers the root causes of hunger strikes and encourages wider sympathy toward the strikers. In the words of Walid Dakka, this political definition is significant for the prisoners' struggle:

> What are we dealing with here? With a definition? Can this or that definition do anything to add or detract from the prisoners' conditions of confinement, or to release those we seek to release? The answer is: Yes! The definition we are demanding is a political definition and not a legal one, and it is not only a theoretical position of principle that derives from it, but also a politically practical one. (Baker 2011, 65)

Defining prisoners' struggles as political is important when negotiating their release. In South Africa, during the last phase of apartheid (1990–1994), there were discussions within South African prisons regarding the definition of political imprisonment. Then-president F. W. de Klerk promised to release all prisoners who were part of once-banned organizations, such as the African National Convention (ANC), but not those convicted of "offenses such as murder, terrorism or arson" (Wren 1990).[4] Whereas the Palestinian Liberation Organization (PLO) signed a deal with Israel as part of the Oslo peace process without achieving the release of all prisoners who defined themselves as political prisoners, South African negotiators had greater success. Members of the ANC, including Nelson Mandela who had just been elected as deputy president, stipulated conditions for any discussion with President de Klerk. These included the unconditional release of all political prisoners. Several resistance groups, including the ANC, called for those who were convicted of violent crimes to also be released.

Just like their counterparts in Palestine and apartheid South Africa, inmates of Guantánamo Bay Detention Camp (established in 2002) are imprisoned without being charged. While the US government insists that their detention is necessary for the sake of national security, it has not provided evidence to support this claim. From George W. Bush through Obama and Trump, the administrations of US presidents and the Pentagon have maintained that it is not legally required to do so, although the courts have not always agreed. What makes Guantánamo distinct in terms of international law is that it is not technically located in US territory and is

---

4   *The New York Times* correspondent Christopher S. Wren quoted the *Sunday Times* archive noting that 350 to 370 of the prisoners were convicted and only 80 to 100 prisoners would be eligible for release. The apartheid regime imprisoned people without conviction, in clear violation of their human rights.

therefore not technically subject to US legal norms (Johns 2005; Hussain 2007). The US Supreme Court (2008) has questioned this interpretation of the law in *Boumediene v. Bush*, yet 41 men remained imprisoned in Guantánamo by the end of the Obama presidency—none of whom were formally charged with any crime. Well into the Biden presidency, the number had only slightly decreased to 37 detainees.

The suspension of legal norms that characterizes Guantánamo as a carceral space means that prisoners have little recourse when their human rights are violated. In this context, inmates have discovered that hunger strikes are one of the few means at their disposal for resisting the conditions of their imprisonment. As early as 2002, prisoners embarked on a hunger strike in response to the removal of a makeshift turban from one of the prisoners. The strike was initiated with 194 participants and concluded successfully when prison guards announced that prisoners would be allowed to wear turbans (Schmitt 2002). However, two hunger strikers persisted with their strike. In response, the guards subjected them to the first known instances of force-feeding in the detention center (Dao 2002).

Both individual and collective hunger strikes continued during the ensuing decade, with a strike in 2005 involving 130 prisoners, at least 80 of whom dropped below 100 pounds (Khazan 2013). In May 2013, 106 of Guantánamo's inmates embarked on a hunger strike. By this point, they had been imprisoned for over a decade, without ever having been formally charged with a crime. In addition to demanding improved prison conditions, the strikers demanded to know the crimes with which they were being charged. Prison authorities responded to this strike by designating a "force-feeding chair," to which inmates would be strapped and forcibly fed. As Ibrahim and Howarth argue, this chair became "ingrained in the aesthetic of power and the necropolitics of invasively keeping the terrorist body alive through torturous feeding rituals" (2019, 295). In 2014, the hunger strikers of Guantánamo won the right to challenge the conditions of their imprisonment, including the practice of force-feeding, through the courts (Pilkington 2014).

Immediate Successes and Larger Effects

In a series of questions in *Strategy of Social Protest*, William Gamson (1990, 28) draws attention to the challenges of measuring success in social movements:

> *Success is an elusive idea. What of the group whose leaders are honored or rewarded while their supposed beneficiaries linger in the same cheerless state as before? ...Is a group a failure if it collapses with no legacy save inspiration to a generation that will soon take up the same cause with more tangible results? And what do we conclude about a group that accomplishes exactly what it set out to achieve and then finds its victory empty of real meaning for its presumed beneficiaries?*

Twenty-four years later, Gamson (2014) reemphasized the difficulty and ambiguity of measuring success in protests and movement actions. In the case of hunger strikes, this difficulty is particularly vivid because they are contextual resistance tactics, with specific, local, and unique concerns. Every hunger strike differs in terms of its demands, place, time, participants, and targets. Strategies that work for one hunger strike do not necessarily work for another. This monograph distinguishes between the immediate impact of prison hunger strikes in helping prisoners achieve their stated objectives and their larger societal effects as part of a broader resistance movement.

A good example of prison hunger strikes having significant effects on a wider movement is the Irish hunger strike of 1981. This seven-month strike achieved some of the Republican movement's aims and brought unprecedented international attention to the struggle for a unified Ireland (Baumann 2009, 178). As one young man after another starved himself to death, the Irish nationalist cause attracted global sympathy. Donations flooded in from around the world. In Britain, this opened up a debate on the constitutional future of the embattled province (Borders 1981). On the ground, the hunger strike of 1981 had an important and lasting consequence for Northern Ireland: it marked a turning point in the Troubles, the guerilla war that persisted for three decades from 1968 to 1998.

Each death-by-starvation inaugurated a new round of street actions, in which supporters of the Irish Republican Army (IRA) threw stones and firebombs in clashes with the police and British troops. The election to parliament of hunger striker Bobby Sands was a milestone in the IRA's resistance struggle and demonstrated the growing support for the hunger strikers and their actions. Sands won office in a by-election during the 1981 hunger strike, less than one month before he became the first Irish hunger striker to die during a strike against Britain (Beresford 1987). Following his death, escalating public resistance became a feature of the conflict and contributed to the electoral rise of Sinn Fein, the political party of the IRA. Whatever their immediate success, these prison hunger strikes were central to organizing civil resistance, institutional political advocacy, and, ultimately, political negotiations between the British government and the IRA.

To the extent that prison hunger strikes bring international attention to domestic carceral regimes, they assist in exposing the many injustices that go beyond immediate incarceration. As such, they are part of broader struggles for self-rule, democratic governance, human rights, accountability of state officials, anti-corruption, prison justice, due process, and equal treatment under the law. The injustices that prisoners experience motivate them to embark on hunger strikes to achieve their demands. Chapter 2 unpacks in detail these motivations and prison resistance more broadly.

Chapter 2. Resistance and Motivations

Documenting the forms and motivations of hunger strikes is fraught with difficulty. Defining whether a hunger strike is performed voluntarily or not, for example, is difficult in custodial settings due to the complexity of the prison facilities as well as the group's peer pressure, which is mostly covert and imperceptible to outsiders. Whether a hunger strike is voluntary, total (limited to the intake of water and salt only), or partial (including sugar and other substances such as honey and vitamins), it is always political and is a radical, last resort act of resistance. This also applies to other types of hunger strikes, such as those that are short-term or open-ended. The latter are usually taken more seriously by both the Israeli Prison Services (IPS) and the community of supporters outside the prison because they are more likely to result in death and thus raise ethical questions about Israeli policies that leave prisoners to die without intervention.

On October 14, 2020, *The Independent* covered the case of 49-year-old Palestinian hunger striker Maher al-Akhras from the West Bank who had been held in administrative detention since his arrest in July of that year. Israel refused to release al-Akhras even as he was "on verge of death" after almost 80 days of hunger striking (Fox 2020). Since death is possible, hunger strikes require commitment, especially for collective strikes. However, these may not be entirely voluntary due to peer pressure, unlike individual hunger strikes that are based on the will of the individual striker.

This chapter focuses on individual and collective strikes. These two forms are the most popular among Palestinian prisoners. Individual hunger strikers usually demand their freedom, an end to administrative detention, or improving their imprisonment conditions. Collective hunger strikers, usually demand an end to practices that affect the prison population in general—especially administrative detention and solitary confinement. Other demands may include better healthcare and access to educational resources, all for more than a single prisoner.

Our interviews, conducted with former Palestinian hunger strikers between 2015 and 2018 in Jordan, Qatar, Palestine, and the UK, indicate that, whether collectively or individually, when strikers had to agree on a single demand, it was liberation, not only from prisons but also from the entire Israeli colonial project that they have been subjected to since birth. To be sure, prison hunger strikers focus on liberation from prison, which for them is a step toward decolonization. Most prison hunger strikers are imprisoned due to their prior resistance, such as taking part in protests and demonstrations as part of the liberation struggle.

According to statistics compiled by the human rights organization Addameer (2022), Israeli prisons contain 4,650 Palestinian political prisoners. Addameer reported that same month that 130 Palestinian prisoners out of 4,650 were from within the territories that since 1948 have been claimed by Israel, 400 were from Jerusalem, 200 from Gaza, and 7 were members of the Palestinian Legislative Council. The collection of statistics on the number of Palestinian prisoners is an activity that Israel regards as hostile to its existence, and as such, the Israeli state has recently tried to stop Addameer's work by classifying it as a terrorist organization (Ayyash 2021).

The reasons for these imprisonments are politically motivated and include joining demonstrations and throwing stones. It is through hunger strikes and other forms of resistance that political prisoners keep the liberation struggle alive, even while incarcerated. This chapter compares individual and collective hunger strikes while analyzing the forms and motives behind hunger strikes.

Types of Hunger Strikes

Hunger striking within prisons has increased over time. Today, prisoners are most likely to use popular resistance, especially protests and hunger strikes. These tactics can be used by most prisoners regardless of physical ability or even the rigor of their confinement, thereby making participation potentially high. In Israeli prisons during the first two decades of the twenty-first century, Palestinians have been more likely to embark on hunger strikes as individuals rather than collectively. Here, hunger striking depends on several factors, including the prison context, Israeli prison authorities' treatment of prisoners, and political opportunities. The following sections explore these dynamics for both collective and individual hunger strikes in more detail.

Collective Hunger Strikes

In 1968, the first collective Palestinian hunger strike did not alter the conditions of imprisonment for those who embarked on it. It was, however, the first political act by prisoners documented by human rights organizations in Palestine (including the Palestinian Prisoner's Society and Addameer). Prisoners used this form of protest to raise awareness regarding their prison conditions. This strike later paved the way for organizing and implementing more effective hunger strikes that achieved their demands. It created a framework within which hunger strikes could become an effective mode of prisoners' resistance that expanded across Israeli prisons (Sarahna interview).

From 1969 to 1976, there were at least six hunger strikes in Israeli prisons. The last strike—which took place in Askalan Prison 13 km north of the border with Gaza—was significant. Forty-five days long, it was both the longest prison hunger strike to date and the first open strike (that is, a strike without a scheduled end date). Earlier strikes had been sporadic and tactical in nature (see Table 2 on page 34 for an overview of collective hunger strikes from 1967 to 2017).

None of the earlier collective hunger strikes freed the strikers, nor did the strikers demand their own release. This is different from liberation in the wider sense, in which prisoners view their resistance—whether through hunger striking or another means—as a step toward liberating and decolonizing Palestine. The interviews conducted with former hunger strikers show that collective strikes brought them better, more humane prison conditions, including noticeably less humiliation and mistreatment. Similarly, subsequent collective hunger strikes also won improved conditions for the prisoners. In a system that is designed to break a person and take away their dignity, any such achievements were for the prisoners a victory and a defeat of the oppressive system.

Collective strikes brought them better, more humane prison conditions, including noticeably less humiliation and mistreatment.

However, the improved conditions still did not meet international human rights standards. For instance, Article 76 of the Fourth Geneva Convention states that prisoners and detainees should enjoy conditions of food and hygiene sufficient to maintain good health. This still does not exist in Israeli prisons. Food poisoning has been documented several times, and the poor quality of food greatly contributes to the declining health of prisoners. In one instance from 1988, prisoners in Ansar III Prison had food poisoning:

> On April 19 it was learnt that about 200 prisoners in Ansar III were suffering from stomach diseases after eating rotten cheese and margarine. Hadashot (April 25) quotes 'military sources at Ansar 111 who tell of dozens of cases of food poisoning from rotten food, and of 15 cases of dehydration due to lack of drinking water. In a letter which the administrative detainees sent to the commander of Ansar III, Colonel Tsemach (Hadashot April 19), they complained that 'we are being given 9 worm-ridden matza because there is not enough bread.' They also complain that the toilets are blocked and flooded with excreta, so that it is impossible to use them. (ROOTS 1988, 9–10)

The annual violation report of Addameer mentions that Palestinian children pay a high price in Israeli prison rooms that "lack proper ventilation and lighting" and who fall victim to Israeli prison authorities' "medical neglect" and "suffer from shortage in food and clothing, isolation and ill treatment" (2020, 104).

The same report mentions the case of Osama Fakhoury, a Palestinian engineering student who was arrested on July 2, 2019, during a house raid. Israeli soldiers "blew off his front door and used military dogs to attack him who tore open the skin just below his knee" (19). A soldier punched him in the face as he left his house, and he was left bleeding the entire time that he was under arrest. The report notes that Fakhoury was subjected to extreme torture in Al-Maskobiyeh Interrogation Center, where he spent approximately 55 days. Furthermore, he was denied proper medical treatment and only received an injection to combat possible poisoning from spoiled or unfit food.

Former prisoner Kamal Abdel Ghazaq al-Rifati reported one incident of mass food poisoning in the late 1980s, involving 22 detainees who were stricken after eating canned meat. "I personally never got fish to eat except for one can of sardines, which was divided among three prisoners. The expiration date written on the can was 1984...." Al-Rifati added that none of the canned meat that the prison authorities give to Palestinian prisoners had expiration dates more recent than 1985. The margarine even dated back to 1982. The prisoners refused to eat all tinned food given to them following the second incident of poisoning (ROOTS 1988, 10).

Whether in Ansar III or other Israeli prisons, jailers are not merely prison staff but also colonizers and oppressors. Table 2 summarizes some of the most notable collective Palestinian hunger strikes between 1967 and 2017, which are discussed in greater detail in this study. All descriptions are based on our original interviews with prisoners and support groups, as well as archives, online resources, and previously published interviews with Palestinian hunger strikers. Palestinian prisoners involved in collective hunger strikes number into the thousands and are too numerous to be named here. It was additionally impossible to list all strikes due to bans on prisoners' communication, security concerns, and the limited flow of information.

Hunger strikes are categorized according to the following five-fold scheme:

- Temporarily successful (the concessions won were later withdrawn)

- Partly successful (prisoners did not achieve all demands)

- Successful[5] (most concessions were won)

- Unsuccessful (none of the concessions was won)

- Made worse (detention conditions became worse following the strike)

In 1976, hunger strikers' collective demands were more broadly focused on general improvements in prison conditions and on giving prisoners access to basic necessities (such as stationery), improving the quality and quantity of food, and regularly replacing plastic sleeping mattresses. In response to the strikers' demands, the IPS implemented some changes. For example, prisoners gained access to stationery, they started managing the prison library, they were permitted to write letters to their families, and forced labor was

---

5   A "successful" hunger strike does not necessarily mean a complete success; it refers rather to achieving most demands on a lasting basis. This categorization depends on the data that the researchers managed to collect for each strike. Thus, errors are possible since not all data was accessible. We also recognize the complexity around measuring and categorizing success in resistance actions, and we adopt the language used by our interlocutors, centering their voices, as they often refer to actions as "successful" or otherwise.

Table 2: Duration, Demands, and Results of Collective Hunger Strikes

DATE	DURATION, LOCATION	NUMBER OF PARTICIPANTS	DEMANDS	OUTCOME	DEGREE OF SUCCESS
28 February 1968	Early 1968, Nablus Prison	(Data unavailable)	1. Provide better portions and quality of food. 2. Stop banning stationery. 3. Stop forcing prisoners to address jailers with the title "My Lord (*ya sidi*)." 4. Allow more than two prisoners to gather in the prison yard at a time. Increase the break time in the yard.	The strike ended when prison authorities put the prisoners in solitary confinement. Hunger strikers were tortured.	* Unsuccessful in achieving most demands * Routine beatings banned for a short period
18 February 1969	8 days, Kfar Yona	(Data unavailable)	1. Permit stationery for writing letters to families. 2. Stop forcing prisoners to address jailers with the title "My Lord."	• Stationery for writing letters was permitted • Prisoners were promised that they would no longer be forced to address jailers as "My Lord." • The promise was subsequently rescinded.	Temporarily successful (the concessions won were later withdrawn)
28 April 1970	8–9 days, Neve Tirza	A hunger strike by women prisoners (Data unavailable)	1. Allow sanitary products provided by the Red Cross. 2. Stop torture.	• Hygiene products were allowed through the ICRC. • Torture did not stop.	Successful
11 December 1976	45 days, Ashkelon	(Data unavailable)	1. Access to stationery. 2. Management of the prison library.	• Access to stationery was granted. • Prisoners were placed in charge of the prison's library.	Temporarily successful
14 July 1980	32 days, Nafha	(Data unavailable)	1. End prison mistreatment. 2. Increase the one-hour break a day.	• Prisoners were forbidden from breaktime, canteen, family, lawyers visits, in addition to lack of medical support.	Successful
23 September 1984	13 days, Junaid, Nablus (in the West Bank), and other prisons	800 prisoners reportedly joined the strike.	1. Books in prisons. 2. Improved ventilation facilities (instead of only small openings in cells). 3. Improved quality of food. 4. Access to radio and television. 5. Civilian clothes. 6. Improved medical support.	• The head of the Israeli Police visited the prison and the strike was called off when demands were achieved. • The head of Israeli Prison Service (IPS) was replaced with Rafi Swisa. • Swisa allowed families to bring night clothes, headphones and recorders. • The provision for the canteen was increased. • Swisa agreed in principle to have a TV in prison.	Successful

Table 2, cont'd

DATE	DURATION, LOCATION	NUMBER OF PARTICIPANTS	DEMANDS	OUTCOME	DEGREE OF SUCCESS
5 January 2000	29–30 days, multiple prisons	At least 650 prisoners participated in the strike.	1. Stop isolation and solitary confinement. 2. Allow unconditional family visits.	• Immediate removal of prisoners in solitary confinement • cessation of strip searches • The promise was subsequently rescinded.	Temporarily successful
15 August to September 2004	17–19 days, multiple prisons	Approximately 4,000 prisoners joined the strikes.	1. Access to phones. 2. Stop strip searches. 3. Removal of glass partitions during family visits.	• Prison authorities responded by removing books, newspapers, cigarettes and salt from the prisoners to punish them. • The authorities stopped family visits. • The hunger strike failed to restore these necessities, with the prison service not making any changes.	Conditions made worse
17 April 2012	The strike was named *al-Karama* (Arabic for "dignity"). In multiple prisons for 28 days.	More than 1,500 prisoners participated.	1. End administrative detention. 2. Allow education. 3. End solitary confinement. 4. Resume family visits. 5. Allow entry of books, newspapers, and clothes. 6. Improve medical care. 7. Resume television channels that were not allowed in prison. 8. Stop strip searches. 9. Stop hand and feet cuffing policy during family or lawyer visits. 10. Stop collectively punishing prisoners with fines.	• The prisoners ended their strike after signing a deal with Israel, mediated by Egypt and the PA, for better imprisonment conditions. • Prisoners were freed from solitary confinement. • The IPS did not fulfil other promises. • All other individual hunger strikers in 2012 were subsequently freed.	Successful

DATE	DURATION, LOCATION	NUMBER OF PARTICIPANTS	DEMANDS	OUTCOME	DEGREE OF SUCCESS
24 April 2014	In multiple prisons, 63 days	Approximately 90 administrative detainees (they were 290 in total) launched this strike to protest their detention without trial or charges.	Protest detention without trial or charges.	• The prisoners ended their strike after a deal with the IPS, with no solid promises. • It was portrayed as a political strike (Netanyahu refused the prisoners' demands. Abbas interfered on the 49th day). • Prisoners were pressured to end their strike because the month of fasting was approaching and there was no clear plan for dealing with it. • The PA intervened against hunger strikers' supporters (al-Nabulsi 2017).	Unsuccessful
17 April 2017	40 days, Multiple prisons	Nearly 1,500 prisoners from across six prisons participated in the hunger strike.	Allow prisoners to take photographs with families.	• The IPS refused to negotiate with the prisoners at the start. • They then agreed to a deal and recognized prisoners' right to education and promised to gradually end solitary confinement. • Unclear if any of these changes have been implemented to date.	Partly successful (prisoners did not achieve all demands)

eliminated. However, a year later the Israeli authorities backtracked on some of these reforms, which led to another hunger strike in 1977. In 1976, hunger strikers' collective demands were more broadly focused on general improvements in prison conditions and on giving prisoners access to basic necessities (such as stationery), improving the quality and quantity of food, and regularly replacing plastic sleeping mattresses. In response to the strikers' demands, the IPS implemented some changes. For example, prisoners gained access to stationery, they started managing the prison library, they were permitted to write letters to their families, and forced labor was eliminated. However, a year later the Israeli authorities backtracked on some of these reforms, which led to another hunger strike in 1977. The strikers created, for the first time, a united leadership that represented all prisoners in all prisons, from Ramleh Prison in the south to Nafha Prison in the north. We know very little about how prisoners communicate. Political scientist Julie Norman interviewed a former prisoner by the name of Nidal who mentioned how prisoners used such communication in early hunger strikes (2021, 84–85). In Nidal's words, when prisoners wanted to organize themselves, they

> started to smuggle... notes between them, from room to room, from person to person: "I plan to do that, what do you think," thing[s] like this, to make a collective step against the Israeli administration. So pens and paper were demands in an early hunger strike.

Beresford (1987) has documented how, in Ireland, prisoners communicated on cigarette and toilet paper. In Israeli prisons, few such stories are documented. In 2014, Angela Davis mentioned a letter she received from the Palestinians (including the Prisoners Movement) in the early 1970s.[6] In the words of Angela Davis, the solidarity message from Palestinian political prisoners "was written on a scrap of paper. A really beautiful message and signatures, and it was smuggled out of an Israeli prison. [It was] given to someone who then brought it to the US and gave it to someone who smuggled it in to me so I could see it" (UCTV 2014).

Letters travel within prisons, between prisons, and outside prisons in ways that only prisoners know. Such letters leave positive impacts on them, even after their release. We see such impacts in prisons around the world, within prisons and between prisons, using all means possible to deliver such letters. When Angela Davis visited Jerusalem with ten Indigenous and women of color feminists between 14 and 23 June 2011, she met one of the former Palestinian prisoners who signed this letter to her. With a smile on her face, she recalled the story:

> I met this older man in Jerusalem who said that he heard that I had told a story about receiving a message from political prisoners in Palestine, and he said that I just want you to know that I was one of the prisoners who signed that message, and it was just so amazing to see that both of us are still involved in struggles for justice today and that we could embrace each other across all kinds of borders: temporal, and political, and cultural. (UCTV 2014)

Since 1968, collective Palestinian hunger strikes have achieved several goals. Stationery, which prisoners used to write messages to their families and friends, used to be unavailable in prisons. Taking pictures and sending them outside prisons was prohibited. The right to own a small radio, to buy and read newspapers, to request specific books, and to take the General Secondary School exam (a requirement to enroll in courses at universities) were all denied to prisoners before the hunger strikes that started in 1968. These rights were all secured through a series of hunger strikes and are examples of successful acts of collective protest. Sometimes, prisoners embark on collective strikes to request the implementation of changes previously agreed on with the prison authorities, as was the case on April 17, 2012, when hunger strikers demanded once again a limit to administrative detention orders—a demand previously made and agreed to.

---

6   This can be seen in two videos noted in the works cited: UCTV 2014, 24:52–26:40 minutes; JVP 2020, 00:00–00:13.

The prisoner leadership only allows prisoners who are in good health to join collective hunger strikes. Those suffering from chronic diseases are not expected to participate. Sometimes, those who are unwell would still join the strike either due to peer pressure or because they prefer to die rather than continue suffering in their confinement. Black Panther Party co-founder Huey P. Newton referred to this practice as "revolutionary suicide" (1973).

Embarking on a hunger strike carries great risks, but the lived experience of imprisonment is as harsh, if not harsher. This shows the severity of the prison conditions that leaves strikers with no other option but to weaponize their lives to live in freedom, even if that freedom is limited to deciding when to embark on strike—"Freedom or death," as prisoners sometimes say (Adnan interview). In addition, the Israeli propaganda apparatus works globally to obfuscate hunger-striking efforts. For example, intravenous treatment is typically forced on hunger strikers, and then may be used to diminish the credibility of the scale of their strike globally. Issawi's sister Shireen stated in an interview (2018) that Samer was compelled to take sustenance intravenously "only when he lost consciousness and was in the recovery room." It was forced on him without his consent. Shireen added that the Israeli authorities attempted to use their publicity about the intravenous (IV) treatment, which deceptively portrayed the prison authorities as moral agents, to diminish the impact of Samer's strike. Such treatment is used to convey that the prisoner is not on a full hunger strike and is taking different forms of food and fluids through the IV treatment.

Collective hunger strikes alter the conditions of imprisonment for the widest number of prisoners. Since they have the greatest immediate impact, they tend to be the most popular and widely practiced type of hunger strike. Yet while they are most likely to secure the greatest leverage and negotiating power for prisoners on strike, sometimes other kinds of hunger strikes may prove more effective. A common alternative that serves more specific ends is the individual hunger strike, discussed in the next section.

Individual Hunger Strikes
Palestinian women and men from various regions and political parties have embarked on individual hunger strikes while in Israeli prisons. Individual hunger striking has been sporadic throughout the history of the Palestinian prisoner movement. So, for example, there are no documented individual hunger strikes occurring between the years 1970 and 1986, or from 2007 to 2009. The demands reflect wider political, social, and economic injustices imposed on prisoners and the wider Palestinian community by the Israeli authorities. Individual hunger strikes have resulted in case-by-case successes, such as release from prisons (Badran and Malasa interviews). Former political prisoners Awni al-Sheikh (who embarked on a hunger strike in 1969), Etaf Elian (who embarked on a hunger strike in 1987) and Khader Adnan (whose hunger strike was in 2005) set the stage for other individual hunger strikes through their pioneering actions. In an interview, Adnan recalled his first experience of striking, saying, "my first hunger strike was very successful. It broke the administrative detention. Prisoners followed me."

When a prisoner embarks on an individual hunger strike, they are often isolated and out-maneuvered by the prison authorities. Adnan noted how the Israeli authorities would "put a camera in your bathroom to break your privacy. They could withdraw your access to a lawyer." Although individual hunger strikes tend to be accompanied by personal demands, their actions are often part of a collective struggle to improve the conditions of their confinement (Sarsak and Adnan interviews). As Adnan shared, "My hunger strike set up a model to deter the occupation. Our aim is freedom and not re-detention. We all are free. We—Ja'far Izzideen and Belal Diyab (individual hunger strikers)—are freed because of our hunger strikes." Table 3 lists five individual hunger strikers' names, the duration of their strikes, and their demands, results, and other details.

Hunger strikes, whether individual or collective, have a deeply sacrificial logic. They involve giving "oneself to the community and the cause and a reciprocation of the community by the reverence and remembrance (through martyrdom)" (Bargu 2011, 3). Thus, even when death is a possible outcome, and even when it is a choice of last resort, a hunger strike is not an act of despair. Rather, a hunger strike, even when done alone, is a political act that is performed on behalf of a collective—whether of an entire oppressed people or of a specific group of oppressed prisoners. The violence of the hunger strike lies more in its potential than in its actuality.

Table 3: Duration, Demands, and Results of Individual Hunger Strikes

DATE	NAME AND DURATION	DEMANDS	RESULTS
25 February 1969	Awni al-Sheikh (150 days)	1. Stop attempting to change the Palestinian curriculum	• Force-feeding • Solitary confinement • Freedom without conditions
1987	Etaf Elian (12 days) Elian embarked on twenty documented hunger strikes, individually and collectively, between 1987 and 2006—probably the largest number of individual strikes among all Palestinian prisoners.	1. The Israeli interrogators tried to pull off her religious headscarf and rip off her dress.	• Attempts by the interrogators to end Elian's strike were unsuccessful until they vowed not to touch her headscarf again. • As she ended her first strike, she was subjected to harsh treatment in all prisons to which she was transferred. • As a result, she declared a second hunger strike through which she demanded to be returned to Ramleh Prison, where political prisoners were held—a demand she later achieved (Shwaikh 2020).
18 December 2011	Khader Adnan (66 days)	1. End her administrative detention	• Freedom on April 17, 2012
16 February 2012	Hana Shalabi (44 days)	1. End her administrative detention	• Freed on April 1, 2012 (but to Gaza, deported on a deal, away from her hometown in Jenin, for three years) • Not allowed back home since then
1 August 2012	Samer Issawi (277 days), the longest-surviving hunger striker in Palestine	1. End his administrative detention 2. Protest his re-arrest 3. Access to secret file of detention (all administrative detainees have such a file) so that he could defend himself	• End his hunger strike in return for a reduction of jail time • Freed on April 22, 2013 • Detained again, six months later and is still in prison (as of August 2020)

The Palestinian Prisoner's Society documented 150 cases of individual hunger strikes between 2012 and mid-2016. Individual hunger strikes have continued beyond 2016 but with less public attention, as discussed in more detail below. The hunger strikers during these five years include Hana Shalabi, Mahmoud Sarsak, Samer Issawi, and Muhammad al-Qiq. What led them to choose individual tactics? Among the relevant factors are the failure of the peace process—demonstrated in the failure of the 1993 agreement between the Palestinian Liberation Organization (PLO) and the Israeli Government to peacefully end the conflict—and the loss of faith in the Palestinian Authority's promise to free all prisoners made during the Oslo Accords negotiations (Peace Agreements 1995).

The following sections unpack stories of male and female individual hunger strikers in Israeli prisons. While this chapter does not deal exclusively with female hunger strikers, the gendered dimensions of hunger striking in Israeli prisons have often been overlooked by scholars and are worthy of careful consideration. From the British suffragettes in the first decade of the twentieth century to Palestinian prisoners in the second half of the century, women have resorted to hunger strikes as they weaponize their lives in unique ways.

Awni al-Sheikh

In 1968, Awni al-Sheikh, then 27, went on the first-documented individual hunger strike in Israeli prisons. The story started when he refused to recognize Israel and its institutions. At the time, he was working as a teacher at the United Nations Relief and Works Agency (UNRWA) in the West Bank. He refused Israeli attempts to change the Palestinian curriculum and chose to not obtain an Israeli ID as required by Israeli law. In the justification of his refusal he stated that the occupation was "temporary" and "illegal."

On 15 September 1968, al-Sheikh was walking alone when an Israeli military jeep approached him and asked for his identity card. He said he did not apply for an identity card and did not recognize the Israeli occupation. He added that he would not have an identity card from them. The Israeli authorities then took him to al-Ramleh Prison. There, they tried to convince him to get an identity card, but he repeated tirelessly, "I do not recognise your existence" (Khamis 2013). The Israeli authorities then told al-Sheikh that he was under arrest, and he was asked to take off his clothing. He rejected, noting that whoever rejects to issue himself an identity card that strips him of his dignity will not take off his clothing in a degrading way. The Israeli soldiers started beating him, breaking his arm.

Al-Sheikh was later transferred to Ramleh Prison where he embarked on an open hunger strike against his imprisonment and the prison conditions that ultimately lasted 150 days. Open hunger strikes, like that of al-Sheikh, are not time-limited; they continue until hunger strikers' demands are achieved. The prison authorities force-fed al-Sheikh while he was on hunger strike—the first documented case of force-feeding in the history of Palestinian hunger strikes.

Al-Sheikh said that the Israeli authorities forced him to "take milk through nose and mouth via the tube to the stomach." There was a lot of "pain, suffering and torture," as he described it. He tried to resist force-feeding but could not stop it (Khamis 2013). The authorities told him that the "process would continue until you stop your strike" (Al-Aissa 2015). After several attempts to resist, he and the authorities agreed that the force-feeding would be done via his nose only. Force-feeding through the nose is more painful, but, for al-Sheikh, it was "more humiliating to open my mouth" and be force-fed that way. Al-Sheikh also said that the prison guards placed him in solitary confinement with no daylight. He was then released from that confinement without further conditions on 15 February 1969. Al-Sheikh nevertheless continued his hunger strike and only resumed eating after his release from prison.

Etaf Elian, Mona Qa'dan, and Hana Shalabi

To better understand women-led resistance actions inside prisons to address incarceration conditions, this section traces solidarity formed among female Palestinian hunger strikes, explores how women dealt with incarceration hardship, and offers a unique angle on prison hunger strikes led by women. Eighteen years after al-Sheikh went on strike, Etaf Elian became the second documented and first female individual hunger striker since 1967. There are fewer women than men in Israeli prisons (Shwaikh 2020).[7] For women prisoners, it is often their first experience in prison. They do not know much about what awaits them behind Israeli prison bars. As Dr. Mithal Nassar (2014) recollected, "My first experience in a prison was strange."

> I was scared and apprehensive. Going into prison, having so many doors locked behind me, being searched and questioned, passing through creepy narrow corridors. I felt this even though I knew I would get out. Hunger strikers don't know if they will be freed or not. I cannot imagine how they feel about their daily lives. No one could, unless they have been there and seen it.

Hana Shalabi (2014) explained her experience:

> The prisoner is taken into a small, cold, dark cell. It lacks basic amenities. The walls are made of rough concrete blocks. If you rub your back against the wall, it feels like glass.

The experience of male and female prisoners in Israeli jails are similar; for example, both are subjected to torture. Yet in other ways, they are different. Whereas Palestinian male prisoners were spread all over Israeli prisons, until 2004, Palestinian women were held in only one Israeli prison: Neve Tirza in the city of Ramleh. This concentration of the female population allowed women prisoners to coordinate their actions more easily.

---

7   As of November 2021, 34 out of 4,650 political prisoners are women.

41

Among the many recorded individual hunger strikes, the most impactful have been those led by Etaf Elian (1987–1997 and again in 2006) who carried out at least 20 hunger strikes, Mona Qa'dan (1999), and Hana Shalabi (2012 for 43 days). The strikes by these three women—

Hunger strikers show clearly how women resist by weaponizing their lives to assert control over their own bodies

the only recorded cases of female-led individual hunger strikers from 1969 until 2004, established a pattern that has subsequently been followed by their male counterparts. To date, female prisoners have been more effective in planning and communicating their actions than men. They have organized their actions more efficiently and achieved more of their demands. Coordination is crucial for individual hunger strikes because it helps them keep the conversation going with other prisoners, especially with prisoners experienced with hunger strikes. This ensures that hunger strikers receive updated information on solidarity actions that raises their morale.

Elian was arrested for the first time in August 1987. This was followed by three other arrests. In total, she spent 14 years in Israeli prisons. Elian's experience is unique in many ways, not only because she was a woman, but also due to her steadfastness in the face of documented beatings and the racial and religious abuse she endured—none of which broke her resolve. She embarked on at least 20 individual and collective hunger strikes between 1987 and 2006, probably more than any other Palestinian hunger striker since 1967.

Following in the footsteps of Elian, in 1999 Mona Qa'dan was the second woman to embark on a hunger strike. In an interview, Qa'dan recalled how she was inspired by Elian's strike from the previous decade. Both prisoners are from cities in the West Bank, Jenin and Bethlehem respectively, and are members of the same political party, the Palestinian Islamic Jihad. Qa'dan's 37-day hunger strike took place while she was being interrogated. She successfully demanded her release. In 2004 during another incarceration, she embarked on a second hunger strike, this time a collective strike with other incarcerated Palestinians who demanded that their families be allowed to visit them.

In 2011, Qa'dan led another individual hunger strike, which lasted 62 days. She was protesting against her placement with the criminal population rather than with other political prisoners. Such strikes, embarked on to obtain the status of political prisoner, characterize the earliest modern deployments of the hunger strike tactic, particularly by suffragettes at the turn of the twentieth century (Miller 2016, 8). Like her suffragette predecessors, Qa'dan demanded to be transferred from the prison cell where she was held with Israeli criminals to the political prisoner section. Eventually, she was granted her request (Al-Laithi 2017).

Elian and Qa'dan inspired other female prisoners to embark on hunger strikes. On February 16, 2012, Hana Shalabi was imprisoned under an administrative detention rule. Following her imprisonment, Shalabi was subjected to violent, humiliating, and hostile treatment, including a strip search. Shalabi's description of this experience underscores the highly gendered nature of this experience, as the strip-searching was performed by male soldiers:

It is very difficult for prisoners to be strip searched. The soldiers make the prisoners undress in front of them. It is difficult for a patriotic Palestinian prisoner to take off his clothes in front of Israeli soldiers. They want to humiliate us, subjugate us. But when they saw us lifting our heads with pride they made other prisoners undress in front of us. I gave them a hard time. I could not accept being strip searched. In front of six soldiers, a nurse and a female soldier. The female soldier let them do it. I tried to fight back but I was handcuffed. My body was covered with scratches from the soldiers' nails. One soldier beat me. He tore off all my clothes by force in front of seven soldiers. This was when I decided to go on a hunger strike and before I was sentenced to six months administrative detention. (Mashharawi 2014, min. 12:00–14:00)

By stripping the bodies of women prisoners, prison authorities endeavor to deprive these women of a sense of control over their bodies and their sexuality. In a conservative society such as Palestine, in which women's bodies are regarded as particularly sacrosanct, the stripping of bodies becomes a prime tactic of humiliating, controlling, and threatening prisoners. It is, therefore, not enough, according to these hunger strikers, to resist the occupation. Palestinian social norms that blame the women for being strip-searched should also be challenged.

In 2018, 17-year-old Ahed Tamimi, a Palestinian activist and former prisoner from the village of Nabi Saleh in the Occupied West Bank, called on Palestinian society to "unify the national struggle and the social liberation movement" to not only free Palestinians from the occupation but also to "fight for a society that has equality and justice between men and women and between old and young" and in which "national activism should be aligned with social activism" (Takruri 2018, min. 5:00–6:00).[8] Hunger strikes are a move in that direction. Women hunger strikers practice dual resistance to both the colonial authorities and the local patriarchal society, reclaiming ownership of their bodies and lives from both systems (Shwaikh 2020; Abdo 2014).

To protest her administrative detention and mistreatment, Shalabi embarked on a hunger strike on the first day of her arrest (B'Tselem 2012). The immediate deployment of a hunger strike may suggest that women hunger strikers go into prison with at least some awareness

---

8   In December 2017, Ahed Tamimi joined a demonstration in her village of Nabi Saleh to oppose the expansion of Israeli settlements near her village. That same day, Ahed's 15-year-old cousin Mohammed Tamimi was shot in the head at close range with a rubber-coated steel bullet. He was then put in a medically induced coma to treat his head injury. Ahed was captured while slapping an Israeli soldier and was detained through the night. The slap went viral and attracted international attention and solidarity with Ahed, who was to serve eight months in Israeli prisons (see Hunter and Atta 2017; BBC 2018).

of the means of resistance available to them. While on strike, Israeli authorities used social pressure to try to stop her strike. An Israel interrogator told her, "You will never get married. You will never get pregnant. Your body will be destroyed. Your society will abandon you" (Shalabi interview). Shalabi persisted in her strike and demanded her release from prison. Forty-seven days into her strike, she finally succeeded in obtaining her release. Under an agreement with the Israeli authorities, she accepted deportation to Gaza. Such seeming concessions are a repressive tactic: no Palestinian deported to Gaza from the West Bank can return to their home.

When Shalabi arrived in her new home, the Gaza Strip, she stated, "I am very happy to be in my country with my people" (Ryan 2015, 117; Shalabi interview). Hunger strikers like Elian, Qa'dan, and Shalabi show clearly how women resist by weaponizing their lives to assert control over their own bodies. Refusing to eat means rejecting the authority of the prisons and jailers as well as the settler-colonial state as a whole. Female hunger strikers have resisted not only the Israeli matrix of power but also a patriarchal society that confines their role to the domestic sphere (Shwaikh 2020). We now turn to the case of an entire family of political prisoners, and of two siblings in particular—one of whom staged the longest Palestinian hunger strike to date—to show how resistance is learned and passed on across generations of prison hunger strikers.

Khader Adnan

In December 2011, Khader Adnan, a baker from Jenin in the north of the West Bank, started what he called "a pattern." By pattern, Adnan meant that he provided an example that other prisoners could follow. He was successful in achieving his demands and gained his release from prison. In the same year, a trend developed: individual prisoners embarked on hunger strikes, demanding their release from prison. In contrast, collective hunger strikes that also took place during those years (starting from early 2011) aimed at improving prison conditions for all prisoners. This pattern of individual hunger strikes demanding release from prisons solidified over time. In 2017, the Palestinian Prisoner's Society, a non-government organization founded in 1993 to support and represent Arab prisoners in Israeli prisons, documented 150 individual hunger strikes between 2012 and mid-2016. These strikes have been criticized by other prisoners for failing to broaden the solidarity movement with prisoners beyond the individual. In an interview, ex-prisoner Anas Abu Khudair stated:

> *Individual hunger strikes are numerous. Some have achieved significant demands. Examples include Samer Issawi, Ayman al-Sharawna, Mohammed al-Qiq, and Khader Adnan. But some have not. This is because of the exhaustion that such political protests produce. Even if there is a solidarity movement supporting a hunger striker, it comes late.... In a political party [like Hamas], embarking on an individual hunger strike is not*

allowed—the reason is that these factions [like the Palestinian Islamic Jihad] have been depleted by this sort of strike. In many cases, individual hunger strikers are administrative detainees who have been sentenced for six months but could have their detention extended beyond one or two years.

Hunger strikes by administrative detainees, as referenced above by Abu Khudair, aim to prevent the extension of prison administrative sentences or to have their detention brought to an end. They contrast other hunger strikes that make different demands, such as improving imprisonment conditions.

The failure of the peace process and the loss of faith in the Palestinian Authority's ability to free all Palestinian prisoners, as reflected in the Oslo Accords, led to an increase in individual hunger strikes, mostly to demand release from administrative detention (Sarsak and Shalabi interviews). Arguably, the most remarkable post-2011 hunger strike is that of Samer Issawi (b. 1979). Issawi carried out the longest hunger strike in the history of the Palestinian prisoners' movement. In the next section, we turn to the story of Samer and Shireen Issawi, siblings from Jerusalem who both experienced Israeli detention and embarked on hunger strikes.

Samer and Shireen Issawi

Having lost their faith in state promises and processes, prisoners took to using their own bodies. Among the most remarkable post-2011 hunger strikes is that of Samer Issawi, who carried out the lengthiest hunger strike in the Palestinian prisoners' movement history, from August 2012 to April 2013; it lasted 277 days. Yet, his strike did not occur in isolation. Issawi comes from a long line of political prisoners, and his sister Shireen also embarked on a hunger strike while in prison. In an interview, Shireen attested to the impact of her brother's actions on her decision to embark on a hunger strike while in prison. Herself a practicing lawyer and a former prisoner, Shireen was arrested five times on various charges. Her last detention was for four years, after she was charged by Israeli authorities with the crime of circulating letters from Hamas prisoners.

During the campaign to free Samer Issawi, in which his sister, Shireen, played a leading role, many of his letters circulated on social media. Some even appeared in mainstream media such as *The Guardian* newspaper, but many others exist only in Arabic or Hebrew languages while some have been lost. Given that Issawi's hunger strike has only begun to be discussed in scholarship,[9] this study has relied primarily on ephemeral sources from social media and the internet to reconstruct Issawi's narrative, drawing on his letters from prison as well as interviews with his sister.

---

9   For exceptions, see Azoulay 2019: 530–1; Shalhoub-Kevorkian 2015: 185; Ajour 2021: 268.

"My story is no different from that of many other young Palestinians who were born and have lived their whole lives under the Israeli occupation," Issawi notes in an open letter (Issawi 2013b). Born in east Jerusalem, Issawi grew up in a family that had experienced the injustice of the Israeli state at its most brutal. At the age of 17, he was arrested for the first time and jailed for two years. As he noted, his family history of political resistance extends back two generations and includes his siblings:

> My grandfather, a founding member of the PLO, was sentenced to death by the British Mandate authorities, whose laws are used by Israel to this day to oppress Palestinians. He escaped hours before his execution. My brother, Fadi, was killed in 1994, aged just 16, by Israeli forces during a demonstration in the West Bank following the Ibrahimi Mosque massacre in Hebron.

Hebron's Ibrahimi Mosque massacre was perpetrated by the American-born Israeli settler Baruch Goldstein who attacked Palestinian worshippers.[10] This act of terrorism led to numerous security measures enacted to seemingly protect Palestinians but which had the opposite effect of further punishing them, with closures and curfews that resulted in job losses, and the denial of medical treatment due to the impossibility of leaving the West Bank (Hass 2014, 73, 248).

Issawi continued in the footsteps of his siblings, who were imprisoned due to their political activities: "Medhat, another brother, has served 19 years in prison. My other brothers, Firas, Ra'afat and Shadi were each imprisoned between 5 to 11 years." He then references his sister, Shireen, who was "arrested numerous times and has served a year in prison." Issawi concludes with pride: "My family, along with the people of my beloved city of Jerusalem, are continuously harassed and attacked, but they continue to defend Palestinian rights and that of the Palestinian prisoners."

Issawi was arrested in 2002, in his early 20s, at the height of the second intifada. He was sentenced to 30 years in prison due to his "resistance to the occupation" (Issawi 2013b). Ten years later, he was freed under an agreement reached between Israel and Hamas, mediated by Egypt, in exchange for the release of Israeli soldier Gilad Shalit (Horowitz, Ratner, Weiss 2011, 217). After his release in 2011, he was subjected to several forms of harassment, including multiple detentions. "During the first month of his release, he was arrested more than once while traveling inside Jerusalem. He was detained for up to 10 hours in police stations and interrogated," his sister Shireen recalled in an interview. He was re-arrested in July 2012. Issawi was the first Jerusalemite freed under the Shalit deal to be re-arrested on the basis of confidential administrative documents that were never shown to him. Issawi was then indicted in the Magistrate's Court of Jerusalem on a variety of charges, the most significant of which was

---

10   At the time of the attack, Goldstein was a resident of the Israeli settlement Kiryat Arba, overlooking Hebron, where the Ibrahimi Mosque was based (Sprinzak 1999, 1–12, 259).

that he had violated the terms of his conditional release (to remain in Jerusalem) by entering the West Bank, a charge he denied. A military committee decided to reinstate the 20 years that remained from his original sentence.

When in prison. Issawi declared a hunger strike on August 1, 2012, to protest his re-arrest and to demand access to the sealed files that had served as the basis for his sentencing, which he had not been permitted to see. He stated that: "I will not wait for another Shalit. I will claim the freedom [that was once denied to me] due to the occupation's failure to honor its commitments. I will do so by a hunger strike" (Qwaider 2013). With this declaration, which his sister Shireen helped circulate around the world, Issawi emphasized that when deals to swap Israeli soldiers with Palestinian political prisoners fail to release all prisoners, they seek freedom through other means. In a letter composed on 3 April 2013, eight months into his strike while he was abstaining from food and speaking, Issawi (2013a) sums up the ironies and contradictions of the administrative detention regime that enables the authorities to imprison thousands of Palestinians without justification. Letters such as Issawi's often make their way outside the prisons through lawyers, as the Palestinian cases discussed in this monograph show.

In words that have come to be referred to by Palestinians as Issawi's "hunger speech" and which circulated widely on social media and on international websites such as *Common Dreams* and *Mondoweiss*, he states, "I am Samer Issawi...the Jerusalemite, who you arrested without charge.... I, who will be tried twice for a charge without charge, because it is the military that rules in your country, and the intelligence apparatus that decides" (Shalhoub-Kevorkian 2015, 185). Issawi's use of the second-person voice (evident here in the words "you arrested" and "your country") is striking and sets his letters apart from other works in this tradition. This rhetorical device de-centers Issawi while showing how Palestinians are transparent about what can get them closer to achieving justice in their struggle. In Issawi's letter, we hear "a call to Israelis to liberate themselves from their own prison, the prison of the jailers, and claim the right to cease being perpetrators" (Azoulay 2019, 530).

Issawi goes on to indict not just the military and the Israeli authorities, but the entire Israeli civil society, including traditionally progressive voices. He notes that "all other components of Israeli society...sit in a trench and hide in a fort that keeps what is called a purity of identity—to avoid the explosion of my suspicious bones" (185). Issawi concludes with an even more direct indictment of Israeli civil society: "I have not heard anyone of you interfering to stop the loud wail of death, it's as if every one of you has turned into gravediggers and everyone wears the military uniform: the judge, the writer, the intellectual, the journalist, the merchant, the academic, and the poet. I cannot believe that an entire society was turned into guards that preside over my death or life, or guardians that protect settlers who destroy my olive trees" (185). With this letter, Issawi issues his own indictment of Israeli society for its complicity in the incarceration of countless Palestinians. Issawi's rhetorical framing suggests that Israeli society has become eroded from within.

Nine months into his strike, Issawi suffered severe deterioration in his health. The Israeli Prison Services threatened him with force-feeding. As reported by his mother, he was also tortured and given a drug that made him faint:

On December 9, my son was given medicine by the Israeli prison authorities and lost consciousness as a result and did not wake up for 48 hours. Also, on December 13, my son was attacked brutally three times inside the courtroom and in front of the judge where soldiers kick their feet on his chest. (Ra'afat interview; Shwaikh 2013)

Shireen Issawi noted that the hospital defended itself against these charges, claiming that they administered the drug to Issawi by mistake. However, according to her, "There is no doubt that they want to kill him."

Issawi felt pain in his whole body and head. Due to pain in his leg, he was unable to sleep on his back. Eventually, to put further pressure on the prison administration, Issawi stopped drinking water, taking vitamins, or having medical examinations. In late 2012, Samer's mother summarized his medical condition:

My son drinks water only, without any solvents or sugar.... He has recently started suffering from severe pain especially in his muscles, abdomen and kidneys. He has an acute vitamin B-12 deficiency and his body has begun to eat his muscles and nerves. Also, his sight is weak, he is fainting around six times a day and his body is covered with bruises. Moreover, he is vomiting blood, his heart is weakening, and he can barely breathe. He has begun to feel pains in his chest due to having been assaulted by Israeli police at his latest court hearing on December 13.... He has not had the necessary tests conducted on him after that attack against him and so far, the hospital administration has refused to test and x-ray his chest. His health continues to deteriorate, his body is eroding, and he has lost a sense of feeling in his extremities [the hands and feet] as well as in his lips and he has lost a great deal of hair. (Ra'afat interview; Shwaikh 2013)

On April 23, 2013, the Israeli Military Prosecution acceded to Issawi's demand for his release eight months from then, on December 23, in exchange for stopping his strike.

The important role played by domestic and international solidarity in Issawi's struggle for freedom shows that the hunger striker never acts alone. Even when embarking on an individual hunger strike, hunger strikers do so on behalf of the collective of which they are a part. Such individual strikers seek to amplify other prisoners' voices alongside their own by demonstrating and receiving solidarity. Like collective hunger strikes, individual strikes raise awareness concerning conditions within the prison. In the case of Issawi, his individual strike was coordinated with people outside the prison who embarked on hunger strikes in solidarity with him. These strikes are a unifying factor in Palestinian politics and the national narrative, both of which are exemplified in the case of Khader Adnan. His wife and children camping outside the prison hospital from where he was striking was broadcast on social media and led to many protests and sit-ins outside the Israeli hospital, all of which led to his freedom.

The threat of Issawi's death, combined with mounting domestic and international pressure reflected in widespread media coverage, compelled the Israeli authorities to reconsider their position. Issawi's hunger strikes have set an example for many Palestinian prisoners. Issawi not only employed hunger strikes but also noncooperation with the Israeli prison authorities (including his "hunger speech" when he did not comply with or answer authorities' interrogations). Issawi's story shows that incarceration, oppression, and confinement may culminate, if only occasionally, in a story of victory.

Issawi's strike also tells another story, one about solidarity from his family members—some of whom were also former prisoners. As Issawi affirms in numerous letters, his tenacity as a hunger striker was not achieved in isolation. Issawi belongs to an activist family, and he has inspired his siblings to follow his example by embarking on hunger strikes when they were in prison. In the case of Issawi, those on the outside—often sisters, mothers, and wives—play a crucial role in the story of every hunger strike. This is, in part, why we have chosen to narrate the stories of Shireen and Samer Issawi together: their hunger strikes form an intertwined narrative.

From the beginning, Issawi's battle was fought with courage. As he noted in a letter to his lawyer on December 30, 2012, "My detention is unfair, and my demands are nothing but just. I will not withdraw from the battle for freedom. I am waiting for either victory and freedom—or martyrdom." Issawi was also able to achieve many of his demands—the ultimate one being his freedom—through the support of his family, including his sister Shireen, who used her legal training to support Issawi's struggle for freedom. In the best tradition of civil resistance, Issawi received support and guidance from his entire community. The domestic and international support he received made it easier for him to persist in his strike. In one letter Issawi sent from prison, he wrote, "I draw my strength from all the free people in the world who want an end to the Israeli occupation. My weak heartbeat endures thanks to this solidarity and support; my weak voice gains its strength from voices that are louder and can penetrate the prison walls" (Issawi 2013b).

Table 4: Comparison of Individual and Collective Hunger Strikes

DIFFERENCE	INDIVIDUAL HUNGER STRIKES	COLLECTIVE HUNGER STRIKES
Actors	Individual prisoners	Collective bodies of prisoners
Demands	Protesting humiliation (case 12), releasing from prison (case 21), and ending imprisonment without charge or trial (administrative detention) (cases 27, 28 and 30).	Providing better portions of food (case 3), improving the ventilation system (case 4), allowing stationery and clothes (case 5) to protesting administrative detention (case 31), and allowing prisoners to take photographs with families (case 32).
Examples	Examples include: Mona Qa'dan (case 21), Khader Adhan (case 27), Hana Shalabi (case 28), and Samer Issawi (case 30).	Examples include: 25 February 1969 (case 2), 25 March 1987 (case 11), and 17 April 2017 (case 32).
Locations	It takes place in one prison cell.	It may take place in one prison cell, more than one prison cell within one prison, or multiple prisons.
Durations	The longest hunger strike in Palestinian history was individual: 277 by Samer Issawi (case 30).	From 1 days (on 18 November 2007, case not included in Table 2) to 45 days (case 7).
The first documented strike	It was first documented on 25 February 1969 (case 2).	The first documented was in 1968 (specific date unknown) (case 1).
Number of strikers	It is embarked on by one prisoner, though there may be simultaneous individual hunger strikes in which the strikers are not coordinating with each other.	A collective hunger strike involves the majority of prisoners (different from a general hunger strike which involves all prisoners).
How are demands chosen?	It is the individual hunger striker's decision.	It usually involves a joint declaration by a prisoners' committee, often after several meetings before reaching the hunger-striking starting point.
Declaration of the strike	The hunger striker sets the demands and the tone of negotiations.	The strike is declared collectively, and a collective body of hunger strikers sets the demands and the tone of negotiations.

The ethos of necroresistance—whereby prisoners, despite being perceived as the weak element in the prison ecosystem, use their bodies to control how they live and die—animates many hunger strikes. Issawi is no exception. He emphasizes this point in his April 2013 speech addressed to the Israeli public, which references the Jewish holiday of Passover:

> I will die satisfied and having been satisfied. I do not accept to be deported out of my homeland. I do not accept your courts and your arbitrary rule. If you had Passed over in Easter to my country and destroyed it in the name of a God of an ancient time, you will not Passover to my elegant soul which has declared disobedience. It has healed and flew and celebrated all the time that you lack. Maybe then you will understand that awareness of freedom is stronger than awareness of death.

Not every striker can match the tenacity of the Issawi family. Since June 2014, Samer Issawi has been back in Israeli prisons. Samer did not embark on a hunger strike this time, probably because his first long strike impacted his health significantly. Was Issawi's hunger strike a success? In Chapter 6, we address the question of success and effectiveness, and ask how defining these is a challenge for any hunger striker, let alone researchers and activists.

Summary

This chapter examines individual cases of hunger strikes, their dynamics, how they started, and what they achieved. It shows how hunger strikers have different abilities. While a prisoner like Samer Issawi managed to launch the longest hunger strike in Palestinian history, this has not been possible for everyone, whether because of health difficulties, political tactics, or resource mobilization—in other words, the resources available for one prisoner at the time of hunger strike may not be available to another.

The resources, timing of the strike, and the health of the prisoners may be some of the few factors that impact the effectiveness of hunger strikes in prisons. In the next chapter, we explore some of those factors in detail and how they impact hunger-striking actions. The Palestinian hunger strikers discussed here attest both to the range of motivations and demands driving the strikes, as well as to the tradition that connects them all. Having examined a range of different forms of hunger striking as resistance, the next chapter focuses on the dynamics through which hunger strikes start and finish, their impact, and their outcomes.

Chapter 3. Hunger Strikes from Start to Finish

How do prisoners embark on a hunger strike? How do they measure the impact of their actions? What are the most effective ways to bring hunger strikes to an end? This chapter focuses on these questions by tracing the dynamics of hunger strikes from start to finish, whether successful or not. It shows that the process of hunger striking is complicated and contentious. Unlike sudden revolts and ad hoc riots, hunger strikes can be a prolonged and open-ended form of resistance in which the prisoners' power is embodied in their choice of action and in their ability to start and end the protest whenever they think it is the right time to do so. Overall, we aim to understand and assess the process by which Palestinian hunger strikers prepare for, begin, conduct, and conclude their hunger-striking actions while they weaponize their lives and assert ownership of their own bodies.

Planning and Coordination

In any resistance campaign, it is necessary to plan strategically and coordinate consistently, before, during, and after the campaign. Planning and coordinating when employing life-threatening modes of resistance is even more important, not only to manage risks and uncertainty, but also to ensure the campaign achieves its desired results. Although the process of planning and coordination varies from one hunger strike to another, individual and collective hunger strikes share certain tactics, such as announcing their hunger strikes through lawyers and addressing the same communities in their letters to ask for their support (as discussed later in the section). There are, however, several differences in the way hunger strikes are conducted and in their goals. For example, in individual strikes, the planning and coordination process is executed on an individual basis or with the help of a limited number of prison inmates and outside supporters. Collective hunger strikes are more complex and involve a large number of prisoners with different ideologies and demands, and they are often spread across different prisons.

Such differences are not limited to the preparation and coordination stages; they are present throughout other phases, which can be enumerated as follows: having unity among prisoners, strong leadership, sustained participation, and communication strategies), including the initial declaration of the strike. Figure 3 presents these phases according to one possible sequence, although there can be significant variation in the order of phases. These are not simultaneous components of the process, and there are times when strong leadership, participation, and communication strategies may no longer be needed. Individual hunger strikers declare their strikes individually, mostly through their lawyers. Collective hunger strikes usually involve joint declarations by a committee (Shawahna 2013). To better understand the process of planning and coordination, the next two sections examine the culture of hunger strikes in the planning process (with a specific focus on the "awareness sessions" that precede hunger strikes), and the significance of prisoners' letters to the outside world in the coordination phase (letters which focus on different elements of hunger strike, with prisoners asking questions such as how to start, whom to contact, when to contact them, what to do if the authorities refused to negotiate, and what to write in letters).

While Palestinians leave it for individuals to decide whether they want to join in their collective action, elsewhere in the world we can observe a longer process involving the gradual selection of prisoners for hunger strikes. For example, the Irish hunger strike of 1981 led by the Irish Republic Army members who were arrested by the British police (for their involvement in what they referred to as British imperialism) was gradual in nature: seven men were selected by the IRA leadership to take part in the strike, and all were chosen from a list of volunteers. In a documentary by Ashraf Mashharawi (2014), Brendan McFarlane, an IRA hunger striker, explains the gradual strategy further:

> We also developed a replacement strategy for any hunger striker who died. And out of the seventy or eighty names we then went about selecting, for example, who would replace Bobby Sands, who would replace Francis Hughes, who would replace Patsy O'Hara, and who would replace Raymond McCreesh (all hunger strikers in the 1981 strike).... [We] sent a clear signal that if a hunger striker died someone took his place and went into the continuous cycle.

When a hunger striker died, the prisoners who had volunteered to join the strike were called on to replace them. One after another, prisoners replaced each other in succession. For example, Sheehan was called on to replace Kieran Doherty, who died while hunger striking in August 1981. This pattern helped to establish solidarity and to coordinate action among the prison hunger strikers. It also helped to prolong the strike, since people starting at different moments would not die at the same time.

Thaqafa: The Culture of Hunger Striking

"The culture [*thaqafa*] of prison is important," former hunger striker Suaad Genem noted. Defining this culture of hunger strikes is a challenge, however, given that the English word doesn't convey the political dimensions of the original term, which can also mean "heritage." Nashif has described *thaqafa* in the Israeli prison context as "the site for captives to resist the effect of the prison by constructing, through the praxis of writing/reading, a counter-hegemonic symbolic field of action" (2005, 166). *Thaqafa* is the "space between captives that transcended the space of the prisons"; according to Nashif, *thaqafa* "became an empowered site for the

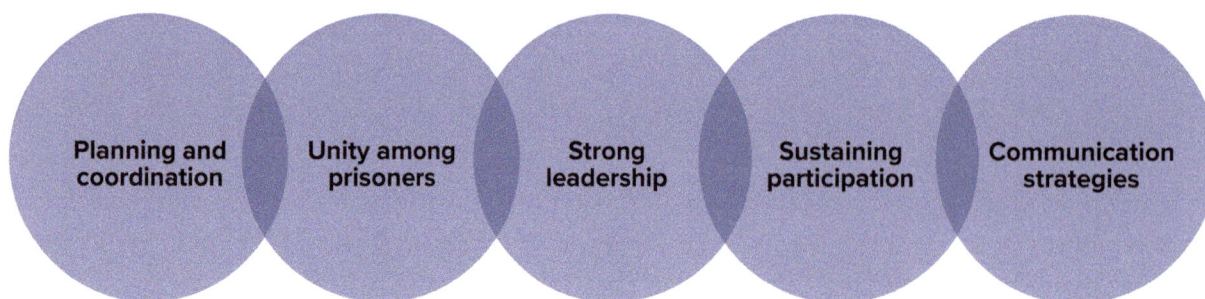

Planning and coordination — Unity among prisoners — Strong leadership — Sustaining participation — Communication strategies

FIGURE 3: THE PROCESS OF HUNGER STRIKES

Palestinians' revolutionary pedagogy" (166). In the context of prison hunger strikes, *thaqafa* encompasses all that prisoners need to keep in mind before embarking on a hunger strike, including what they need to take (in terms of vitamins, water, and milk, if any) and what to avoid (which may include not reading, avoiding sports, or ceasing any other activity which may exhaust them) to ensure their organs function for as long as possible during their strike.

Even before prisoners issue a declaration of a hunger strike, the preparation phase begins. "This is usually done through holding awareness sessions where prisoners meet to discuss their demands and to elect the strike's leaders" (Sarsak interview). Prisoners discuss the logistics of engaging in a hunger strike. How much salt does a hunger striker require for their organs to keep working and to stay alive? And how frequently? How many liters of water do they need to drink in order to stay conscious and for their bodies to survive? What activities do they need to cease to continue with prolonged fasting as part of their resistance? Clearly, there is more to the culture of hunger striking than the strike itself. "Culture" also involves detailed knowledge about how to embark on a hunger strike: what to eat and what not to eat, and how to start and end the protest and succeed.

Awareness sessions are vital for raising the prisoners' morale, exploring the importance of the strike action, and raising consciousness about the strike and its potential impact. These sessions raise awareness about what prisoners can and cannot do while striking. In the words of former hunger striker Mazin Malasa,

> *I have learned from my hunger strikes to drink one to two liters of water daily, and a pinch of salt, to prevent the intestines from going rotten. Also, I cannot move a lot: even reading should be minimized because it is an activity that tires the body. It is also recommended not to face the sun, and not to use a loofah [when washing] because it removes cells from the body.*

Lessons that Malasa and others have learned while hunger striking are shared during these sessions. "Without such sessions, prisoners could easily feel lost. In such sessions,

54

prisoners benefit most when their specific demands and aims are set out for their strike" (Safadi interview).

Former hunger striker Mahmoud Sarsak noted these gatherings are "informal in nature."

Prisoners discuss domestic and international examples of hunger strikes, exploring their demands and outcomes, and factors contributing towards success or failure. They share universal good practices, which raise the prisoners' confidence and improve their knowledge and experience.

During such sessions, Sarsak continued, "prisoners are trained to deal with all potential scenarios." When prison hunger strikers do not have the benefit of knowledge-sharing sessions, the chances of their success—and their lives—are jeopardized.

Mazin Malasa, for instance, noted that during his first strike in 2000, his demand was either to see a lawyer or to be transferred from the interrogation room to a prison cell. Mazin did not go through an awareness session before his first strike. This lack of training quickly brought negative consequences. He "became very thin and suffered severe stomach pains that needed urgent medical assistance." A doctor and a nurse visited him, and he was told that he would die if he did not end his strike. Training in the culture of hunger strikes enables prisoners to deal more effectively with such pressure. Being prepared for the deterioration of their health, especially when the authorities deny them access to medical care, supports their determination to continue the strike.

Thirteen days into Malasa's hunger strike, he was finally granted access to a lawyer. At this point, he ended the strike. He could not continue because he had a limited understanding of what techniques to use to engage in this risky action. Malasa recognized that he had not properly assessed how much salt his body might need: "Instead of taking the small, necessary amount, I took too much." Malasa's hunger strike illustrates the importance of awareness sessions for hunger strikers.

After Malasa ended the strike, the Israeli authorities gave him soup and breadcrumbs. However, this food had a disastrous effect on Malasa's health. He explained the experience:

Only later did I realize that this made my stomach worse. For five days, I was eating, and I had not gone to the toilet—I had severe constipation. I was like a woman with labor pains. Every time I went into the toilet, I cried from pain. My inmates heard me and grew concerned about my health. Later, the nurse came and asked me for a stool sample. I was so angry I threw the sample container in his face. Following a few difficult days, the doctor gave me a suppository. Later and after significant ordeals, things got a bit better, but it was a lesson for life.

Malasa's story demonstrates not only the risks associated with hunger strikes but also that understanding how to manage one's own hunger strike and the strategy behind it are crucial aspects of this complex tactic (Nafie interview).

While Malasa paid a price and then learned from his mistakes, awareness sessions allowed other hunger strikers to know better ahead of time. Ala Hamad's story was told by his wife Muntaha Qassem in a 2016 interview. Hamad, a Palestinian with Jordanian citizenship, was sentenced to 12 years and incarcerated in Israeli prisons beginning in November 2006. He was prevented from receiving family visits for seven years. He was seldom allowed to phone his family. Before embarking on a hunger strike to demand more frequent phone calls with his family, he formally requested access to calls through the Israeli Prison Services (IPS) beginning in 2008. Two years later, his application was accepted. He was then allowed to talk to his family for ten minutes at a time. The prison authorities would permit him to make a phone call, but such occasions were sudden, without advance notice, and he was unable to inform his family so that they could expect his call. At the time of the interview with Qassem in 2016, none of Ala's six children had ever been able to talk to him since his incarceration in 2006.

Understanding how to manage one's own hunger strike and the strategy behind it are crucial aspects of this complex tactic.

When Ala Hamad was imprisoned, his youngest son, Issa, was six months old. In 2016 (when the interview with Muntaha Qassem was conducted), Issa was ten and still had not seen his father since his arrest. In 2010, to protest a lack of permission to phone his family regularly, Hamad embarked on a month-long hunger strike. This particular strike was a success: it secured him the right to call his family regularly. The IPS also gave him books that he requested from them on religion, history, and nonpolitical literature. Unfortunately, Hamad began to suffer from poor eyesight, which was exacerbated by his hunger strike. All that he had been offered to address his health problems before the strike was the over-the-counter fever-reducing medicine paracetamol, so medical treatment became one of the demands of his strike. He eventually received glasses to aid his vision.

The difference between Hamad's and Malasa's hunger strikes is that the former had a better understanding of what it involved. Unlike Malasa, Hamad knew what to eat and what not to eat before and after the hunger strike to maintain his health. When a prisoner has family members, close friends, or colleagues who have been through the experience, they are better prepared to embark on a hunger strike. It is also worth emphasizing the impact of political education within prisons, which can make a prisoner more aware and confident in their action.

Hamad's account demonstrates that hunger strikes are sometimes effective in achieving the intended results, but these achievements can be easily reversed by the authorities. This happened later with Hamad when his regular phone calls with his family were canceled. When prison authorities renege on their promises, prisoners usually embark on different types of resistance, ranging from longer hunger strikes to noncooperation with IPS rules, to regain their rights. Hamad was left with a difficult choice: to embark on another hunger strike, or to stay silent. Hamad initiated a new hunger strike every time his request to call his family was denied (Qassem interview). Hamad's robust health made it possible for him to embark on multiple hunger strikes. Meanwhile, prisoners suffering from physical or physiological disabilities were unable to go on strikes spontaneously.

Unity

Despite the harsh conditions endured by Palestinian prisoners, one key feature of the pre-Oslo period was their unity, which greatly facilitated their efforts to mobilize collective hunger strikes (Dakka 2009; Abu Atwan 2007; Saad 1979). Prisoners' leaders were taken seriously by Israeli jailers, causing one former leader to remark that "they doffed their hats for me" (Genem interview). Another prisoner said that "the Israeli authorities would think twice before speaking to any prisoner. [They first have to] approach our leadership" (Abu Atwan 2007; Abu al-Haj interview). Also prior to 1993, prisoners fought collectively, regardless of their political affiliation or geographical location (Dakka 2009). Their demands were coordinated and mostly collective, ranging from ending solitary confinement and the compulsory use of the designation *ya sidi* ("my lord" or "sir") when addressing prison officers, to gaining access to educational opportunities. That these issues affected most or all prisoners motivated the unity of their protest. When prisoners faced new challenges, they planned, coordinated, and protested together.

The united front created by the Palestinian prisoners' movement reflected the Palestinian struggle outside prisons as well. This movement made it easier for prisoners to focus on the anti-colonial struggle, a point highlighted in their extensive political awareness sessions. As a result, prisons became educational, political, and anti-colonial institutions. In the words of Palestinian novelist Sahar Khalifeh, Israeli prisons became the "people's schools" and were crucial to the coalescence of leadership during the 1970s (Robinson 1997, 22). This situation persisted into the 1980s and the early 1990s. In *Palestinian Political Prisoners: Identity and Community* (2008), Esmail Nashif (2008, 10) translated Lisa Taraki's description of prisons before Oslo:

> *Powerful symbols in the political folklore of the occupied territories, [prisons] are often considered by the "graduates" as the ideal place for acquiring a political education. There, isolated from the routine of normal life, prisoners organized seminars and study*

circles, conducted Hebrew and English lessons, and taught the illiterate among them how to read and write. The impact of this collective experience is no doubt a lasting one.[11]

Freedom from imprisonment was discussed every time Shwaikh met with former political prisoners. One recurring theme is the connection between release from prison and freedom. Many prison hunger strikers who secured their release through their strikes were arrested later. For example, Samer Issawi was re-arrested in June 2014 (IMEMC 2014). He is still in prison as of this writing (June 2022). Similarly, Khader Adnan was re-arrested several times since his 2012 hunger strike, the latest of which was in May 2021 when he began a 25-day hunger strike that secured his release on 28 June 2021 (Al-Mayadeen 2021).

Another aspect of unity relates to a shared commitment among the hunger strikers. Collective prison hunger strikes have greater levels of success when they involved a unified approach among different sectors of the prison population, for example, with trade unionists, activists, and other members of the public striking together.

Leadership

Hunger-striking members of the most influential political movements in South Africa (African National Congress), Northern Ireland (Irish Republican Army), and Palestine (Palestinian Liberation Organization and others) discovered their identity as political leaders while imprisoned. Nelson Mandela and Bobby Sands became elected representatives at the federal level. Other hunger strike leaders were assigned leadership roles by movement members. Marwan Barghouti, once the West Bank General Secretary of Fatah, rose to even greater prominence after his imprisonment on the charge of murder. Barghouti often called for the reform and expansion of the PLO. From Mandela to Sands, the most successful leader of hunger strikes were those who could demonstrate the most extreme devotion to the cause.

In 1977, Palestinian prisoners managed to create for the first time a united leadership that represented all prisoners across all Israeli prisons by developing a sophisticated communication network unknown to the larger prisoner community. The evolution of a unified resistance at this point in 1977 crucially shapes how prisoners demand change and the broader resistance strategies they employ to reach their goals.

During collective hunger strikes, the negotiation process rests on the shoulders of the strike leaders. This will be illustrated by considering the 2004 Palestinian collective hunger strike, which was arguably a failure. To some extent, the divided leadership failed to coordinate and develop a unified strategy for negotiations with the prison authorities. Prisoners gained

---

[11]   Nashif's translation from Arabic has been edited slightly for the sake of clarity.

none of their demands and lost many of the concessions they had previously secured from the prisons (Malasa and al-Faleet interviews). Ending a strike without success can be painful and demoralizing, both for the strikers and the community supporting them. Hunger striker Mazin Malasa, whose story was discussed in the previous section, grasped this dilemma with particular acuity. Having participated in both successful and unsuccessful strikes, he recalled:

> *I felt despair when I failed to achieve my demands. I thought people would not take me seriously. I participated in hunger strikes twice individually and once in a group hunger strike. It is even harder when it is a collective hunger strike. This is because you take responsibility for the morale of many other people. It is harder to be a leader who decides to lead a strike and then fail to accomplish any of the strike demands.*

To push the Israeli authorities to accede to strikers' demands, prisoner-negotiators count on internal and external pressure. Internal pressure comes from other prisoners who continue their hunger strikes during the negotiations. External pressure, by contrast, is generated by those outside the prisons who engage in resistance methods such as protests and solidarity hunger strikes.

Sustaining Participation

Aside from the continuous threat of force-feeding, there is also the challenge of sustaining participation during the strike. As soon as the hunger strike begins, it becomes important to manage and maintain discipline and participation by holding regular meetings and insuring uninterrupted communication among the strikers. Prisoners interviewed for this monograph noted that it is difficult to sustain participation during the first days of hunger strikes (Sarsak and al-Faleet interviews). Hunger striker and political prisoner Loai Odeh reflects on this further:

> *The first day of a hunger strike is the hardest. Abstaining from food or drinks has a great impact on strikers during the first three days. But what distinguishes the first day is the measures that the Israeli Prison Service (IPS) takes against our prisoners, attempting to break them. The jailers confiscate all prisoners' possessions…. They remove everything the cells contain in a very provocative way, damaging a lot of valuable items our prisoners have collected throughout their previous years in jail to ease the pain of their daily lives. On top of that, IPS conducts misinformation campaigns between cells and prisons, so that no one knows whether he will be separated from his circle of friends and the environment to which he has adapted. (Abusalama 2012)*

Former hunger striker Suaad Genem shared similar thoughts:

Starting a hunger strike is more momentous than declaring it (whereas declaring pertains to announcing the strike, starting pertains to stopping food intake). It took the prisoners years to start one. In 1992, the strategic hunger strike took two years of preparation. The difficulty of the first days stems from uncertainty regarding the Israeli reaction to the strike, and the strikers' subsequent response. Sustaining participation at this point is crucial. The prisoners' call for sustained engagement and resilience is encapsulated in their motto: "freedom or death."

Another challenge manifested as early as day one is inconsistency in the number of participating hunger strikers. In other words, hunger strikers may need to wait until the end of the first day of the strike to know how many have joined them. Then there is the challenge of the frequent and uncoordinated wave of individual on-and-off strikers. For example, the 2014 collective hunger strike in Israeli prisons started with 125 political prisoners and ended with 80 (Khoury 2014). Dropouts are expected in a hunger strike given how harsh it is to undertake them. This inconsistency has occasionally obstructed the broader prisoners' movement and has lessened the confidence of observers and participants regarding the seriousness of the prisoners' actions (Shawahna 2013). This is also vexing to supporters who may find it hard to keep track of on-and-off protests.

Israeli repression, however, is not always sufficient to bring hunger strikes to an end. Repression can backfire. Prison hunger strikes have increased over the years, exemplifying what Banu Bargu (2014) refers to as "necroresistance," whereby prisoners use their bodies to control how they live and die. This takes place regardless of the social and political power that states have to dictate life and death, which Bargu calls "necropolitics." Prisoners' growing participation in hunger strikes also aligns with Brian Martin's (2006) concept of backfire.[12] The use of violence by the Israeli authorities to pressure hunger strikers to stop their actions can negatively impact Israel's global image, making it more difficult for the Israeli state to present itself as being compliant with international law and a beacon of liberal democracy.

Communication Tactics

A hunger strike without publicity is a silent hunger strike. For the hunger strikers, it is important to let people outside the prison know that they are embarking on a strike. The resources at their disposal are quite limited, and prison authorities often make it harder to get their voices heard beyond prison walls. Letters are among the most important tools used by prisoners to

---

12   The backfire framework of Brian Martin can be used to understand tactics of perpetrators of injustices and the ways to oppose them. Political actions backfire when they are widely perceived as unjust and are effectively communicated broadly to significant peoples.

communicate their demands and involve the international community. The role of letters attracting the international community to the strikers' cause is explored further below. It is important to note here that letters—especially public ones—are just one part of a much larger communication network. They can develop into a strategic tactic alongside which unauthorized phones are used to send and receive communication from outside and within prisons.

Prisoners' Letters to the Outside World

It is very important that a hunger strike has as much publicity as can possibly be generated for it. So, for example, there is no point for going on a hunger strike if no one knew about it because the whole point is to use it to bring pressure on your political opponent. (Sheehan 2014)

These words from former Irish hunger striker Pat Sheehan testify to the importance of communicating to the outside world during strikes. In Palestine, it may be true that, even without outside pressure, one aim is to make the internal prison system unworkable in order to force prison authorities to negotiate with hunger strikers. Still, prisoners' letters to the outside world, to their families, and to supporting communities, declare hunger strikes and provide updates on the hunger strikers' conditions. Continuing a long tradition of prison writing in epistolary form,[13] prison hunger strikers' letters aim to raise support and promote solidarity from domestic and international audiences.

In Iran, letters from prison have often shaped outside observers' perceptions of prison conditions and helped form networks of solidarity. Iranian political prisoner Shahrokh Zamani used letters to spread his message concerning prison conditions and unjust imprisonment. He also appears to have been more harshly punished as a result of these writings (Amnesty 2014). Letters from Iranian political prisoner Nasrin Setoudeh have been published by the Center for Human Rights in Iran (CHRI) and Amnesty International, in which she announced her strikes and protest against the general condition of prisoners in Iran (Setoudeh 2020). These drew attention to the impact of her imprisonment on her family (Setoudeh 2019a) and appealed to the outside world (Setoudeh 2019b).

Palestinian hunger striker Samer Issawi's multiple letters from prison also belong to this epistolary tradition. In one of his public letters (2013a), he addresses the Israeli public:

I am Samer Issawi on hunger strike for eight consecutive months, laying in one of your hospitals called Kaplan. On my body is a medical device connected to a surveillance room operating 24 hours a day. My heartbeats are slow and quiet and may stop at any

---

13   Prior examples of prison writing in the form of letters include King 1968; Gramsci 1971; Michnik 1986.

minute, and everybody, doctors, officials and intelligence officers are waiting for my setback and my loss of life.

I chose to write to you: intellectuals, writers, lawyers and journalists, associations, and civil society activists. I invite you to visit me, to see a skeleton tied to his hospital bed, and around him three exhausted jailers. Sometimes they have their appetizing food and drinks around me.

The jailers watch my suffering, my loss of weight and my gradual melting. They often look at their watches, asking themselves in surprise: how does this damaged body have an excess of time to live after its time?

In the same letter, Issawi continues:

I am Samer Issawi the young "Arboush" man according to your military terms, the Jerusalemite, whom you arrested without charge, except for leaving Jerusalem to the suburbs of Jerusalem. I, who will be tried twice for a charge without charge, because it is the military that rules in your country and the intelligence apparatus that decides, and all other components of Israeli society ever have to do is sit in a trench and hide in the fort that keeps what is called a purity of identity—to avoid the explosion of my suspicious (or "questionable") bones (or "flesh" or "existence").

I have not heard one of you interfere to stop the loud wail of death, it's as if every one of you has turned into gravediggers, and everyone wears his military suit: the judge, the writer, the intellectual, the journalist, the merchant, the academic, and the poet. And I cannot believe that a whole society was turned into guards over my death and my life, or guardians over settlers who chase after my dreams and my trees.

In the concluding part of this letter, Issawi adopts a hortatory tone, stirring his readers not just to action but to upright lives:

Listen to my voice, the voice of our time and yours! Liberate yourselves of the excess of greedy power! Do not remain prisoners of military camps and the iron doors that have shut your minds! I am not waiting for a jailer to release me. I'm waiting for you to be released from my memory.

Hunger strikers' letters typically emphasize ethics, justice, and morality. First, demands are phrased in clear and moving language, making it easy for anyone to understand them, no matter how limited their knowledge of the prisoners' conditions. Through letters, prisoners look for all sorts of support or understanding, from individuals and groups. In a letter published by *The Guardian*, Issawi (2013b) writes:

Do not worry if my heart stops. I am still alive now and even after death, because Jerusalem runs through my veins. If I die, it is a victory; if we are liberated, it is a victory, because either way I have refused to surrender to the Israeli occupation, its tyranny and arrogance.

In these words, Issawi looks beyond political polarization. His words are directed to those who support the Palestinian cause as well as those who choose to stay neutral or oppose it. Such letters identify or define goals behind the hunger strike in order to bring them within reach. Issawi's letters are striking. He uses rhetorical devices that center his narrative while also showing how the story is about more than himself. All Palestinian prisoners and hunger strikers are involved in the anti-colonial struggle. Even more strikingly, his letters include a call to Israelis to liberate themselves from their own colonial structures, as the next chapter explores. Of course, more tools may be available to prisoners and their supporters. For example, social media has been used to amplify hunger strikers' narratives and debunk those of the Israeli prison authorities. Prison resistance, including innovative modes of communication within and outside the prison, generates further prison repression, which is the focus of the next chapter.

Chapter 4. Prison Repression

This chapter addresses Israeli state repression against Palestinian prisoners and explores how force-feeding has been historically used and challenged, the ethical and moral questions it poses, and how it attracts worldwide interest. It also examines remote prisons, used by colonial and authoritarian prison authorities to cut prisoners off from the rest of the world. We also note other prison repressive measures, some of which include banning all communication, which is important to bring support and solidarity to hunger strikers. This chapter concludes by detailing how prisoners react to such forms of repression, and how their resistance continues from within prison.

Force-Feeding

Writing of a hunger strike in Guantánamo Bay Detention Camp in March 2013, Ian Miller (2016) notes that hunger strikes pose "a formidable moral question: Is it acceptable to allow a prisoner to starve to death?"

> *Corpses present problems. A dead hunger striker can offer evidence of deplorable prison conditions. A death also goes some way towards validating dissident political perspectives. These, after all, had been worth dying for.*

At the height of their protest, 106 individuals were refusing to eat. As Miller noted, for detainees incarcerated for over a decade without charge or trial, food refusal offered a "potent way to rebel" (2009, 1), defying the government that incarcerated them and drawing international attention to the institutional violation against them. Their hunger strike magnified the possibility of their death and posed questions about the ethics of force-feeding. Such questions are important to the authorities, for whom corpses present ethical and moral dilemmas internally and on the international stage.

As soon as prisoners embark on their hunger strikes, the pressure to push them to end their strikes begins, and it increases with time. It is important to address force-feeding in the context of our strategic look at a hunger strike. Force-feeding is a form of physical and psychological torture used to prevent prisoners from peacefully demanding their rights (Boumediene 2017). First used in a systematic way against the British suffragettes at the turn of the twentieth century (Miller 2009), force-feeding has become normalized by various carceral regimes, even though, when administered by doctors, it is a violation of the Hippocratic oath.

States defend force-feeding on the grounds that it "saves lives," yet this practice carries significant medical risks and can contribute to a prisoner's death, as in the case of Irish revolutionary and hunger striker Thomas Ashe, who died in 1917 at the age of 32 after being force-fed by British prison authorities (Ashe 1917; O'Casey, O'Connor, and Lang 1918). In 1980, the Israeli prisons used force-feeding through plastic tubes against hunger strikers, resulting in the deaths of Rasem Halaweh Ali Jaafari and Anas Doula. According to hunger striker Suaad Genem, "constant voluntary feeding has been used in Israeli prisons since hunger strikes were first initiated. Voluntary feeding was not done through tubes. Rather, prisoners would decide, if they were offered milk supplements [by the prison authorities], whether to take them. Prisoners have refused force-feeding but they have accepted voluntary ones."

Force-feeding was first documented in Israeli prisons following the Six-Day War. As documented in Chapter 1, it was used against hunger striker Awni al-Sheikh in 1969 (Al-Atrash 2015; Sarahna interview). He was forced to "take milk through the nose and mouth via the tube to the stomach" (Khamis 2013). Later that year, prisoner Rasmiya Odeh, who had initiated a hunger strike with other women prisoners to demand better treatment, was also force-fed. In her own words, the Israeli authorities "fed us by force, with tubes through our nostrils. Two girls were taken to the hospital and until today one of them still has trouble with her stomach and the other with her nose" (Antonius 1980, 50). Several other cases were documented while conducting this research (see Tables 2 and 3 on pages 34 and 39, respectively), but until 2015, force-feeding was implemented outside official regulations. It was conducted forcefully, resulting in three hunger strikers dying during or shortly after being force-fed (Claiborne 1980; Jaradat 2011).

Palestinian hunger strikers also recall how force-feeding is used to degrade and dehumanize them. Palestinian hunger striker Moussa Sheikh, who was force-fed in 1970, explained:

The prisoner enters the room handcuffed and legs shackled. There are two police officers on either side of the prisoner, who terrorize him physically and mentally. They poke him harshly in the ribs and on the back of the neck, talking the whole time in a way... meant to break the prisoner's spirit, saying things like "You are practically dead now." The prisoner is tied to a chair so that he [cannot] move. The doctor then sticks the tube up the nose of the prisoner in a very harsh way. When it was done to me, I felt my lungs close as the tube reached my stomach. I almost suffocated. They poured milk down the tube, which felt like fire to me. It was boiling. I could not stay still from the pain. (Alsaafin 2015)

The Israeli authorities claim that force-feeding is used as a last resort to save hunger strikers' lives. Yoel Adar from the Israeli Public Security Ministry claimed that hunger strikers can harm the public. When asked how, he said, "If he dies in prison, it causes riots in prison and elsewhere. This has a definite implication for Israel" (IC10 2014).

While prison authorities often neglect prisoners' well-being, they generally will do everything possible to avoid their deaths. This dehumanizing pattern whereby prisoner needs are often neglected while prison authorities claim they are saving lives is a global phenomenon. For example, in Turkey, the justice minister Hikmet Sami Turk justified police raids to end a hunger strike that led to 20 deaths. "It is unthinkable for the state to stand by and watch as people bring themselves face to face with death," he claimed. "The goal of this operation is to save people's lives" (Logan 2000).

Prison authorities tend to overlook the evidence that force-feeding is a violation of medical ethics. In October 1975, the World Medical Association (WMA) adopted guidelines for physicians concerning torture and other cruel, inhumane, or degrading treatment in relation to detention and imprisonment by the 29th World Medical Assembly of Tokyo, editorially revised in 2005, 2006, and 2016. Point 8 of the declaration stipulates:

> *Where a prisoner refuses nourishment and is considered by the physician as capable of forming an unimpaired and rational judgment concerning the consequences of such a voluntary refusal of nourishment, he or she shall not be fed artificially, as stated in WMA Declaration of Malta on Hunger Strikers. The decision as to the capacity of the prisoner to form such a judgment should be confirmed by at least one other independent physician. The consequences of the refusal of nourishment shall be explained by the physician to the prisoner.* (WMA 2022)

In addition to the medical advice against force-feeding, a thorough investigation into the conditions under which Palestinian hunger strikers were force-fed shows they were administered in the first few days of their hunger strike. For instance, Abu al-Fahem was only on his third day of hunger striking when force-feeding began, even though his health condition was not life-threatening (Jaradat 2011). Deaths from force-feeding led to political unrest in Palestine. It is believed that the nasal feeding tubes were inserted incorrectly and most probably into prisoners' lungs instead of their stomachs. Demonstrations were organized and clashes between Palestinian civilians and Israeli soldiers erupted (Issawi interview).

Prison authorities tend to overlook the evidence that force-feeding is a violation of medical ethics.

Along with force-feeding, prison authorities developed other tactics for tormenting prisoners. In a four-hour conversation with Palestinian former political prisoner Suaad Genem in 2017, she recounted some of the ways in which prison authorities mock and torment prisoners:

> *Along with force-feeding, Israeli authorities tend to divide leaders, torturing them, putting them in solitary confinement. The Israeli authorities will then eat the strikers' best food in front of them, in an attempt to harass them. But the morale of the prisoners is strong.*

After ten days or so, the hunger strikers become very thin and light, and they cannot feel their head, and their muscles become sore, and they try to stop talking about food. It is what they talk about more than anything else; they imagine and dream about food.

To survive Israeli violence, Genem added with reference to collective leadership that "it is important to stay strong" and to act "as if nothing was happening that might surprise the Israeli authorities." Subsequently, the use of force-feeding was halted by an order from Israel's High Court in 1980 (Abusalama 2017; Hamdouna interview). This highlights two significant points. One is the importance of popular and sustained Palestinian pressure on the Israeli colonial authorities to achieve hunger strikers' demands and to stop force-feeding. The other is global solidarity with hunger strikers and their push against inhumane treatment that made halting force-feeding a possibility. Any unrest has the potential to attract the world's attention and can impact Israel's security, which is often a red line for the regime's calculated actions. The use of force-feeding was then legalized in June 2015, and it was first used against hunger striker Mohammed al-Qiq while protesting his administrative detention on January 12, 2016. Al-Qiq finished his 94-day hunger strike on February 26, 2016, after agreeing with the Israeli authorities on a date of freedom of May 21, 2016. He was freed on May 19, 2016.

Remote Prisons in the Negev

The Israeli prison authorities have used remote prisons in Palestine, more specifically, in the heart of the Negev desert. This location presents a challenge to prisoners' survival, cutting them off from their families and supporters, as a document published in 1988 by Roots and Friends of Palestinian Prisoners explained. In the report, the Negev desert was depicted well: "There are no television cameras here to record the breaking of bones. There are only scorpions, snakes and flies and the eyes of 3,500 Palestinians—who record everything, who remember everything" (ROOTS 1988, 4; see also Kawas 2020).

Ansar III Detention Centre in the Negev was opened March 22–25, 1988, but as the document shows, its story dates back to June 1982 when Israeli forces invaded Lebanon and moved north to besieged Beirut, rounding up all males between the ages of 14 and 60, comprised largely of doctors, lawyers, teachers, civil servants, and students. Those tens of thousands of detainees were held in camps in South Lebanon, called Ansar, with conditions similar to the ones prevailing in Ansar III: "barbed wire, soldiers with machine guns and tanks, opening fire with little or no provocation, persistent brutalization of the detainees, horrid sanitation facilities, virtually no medical care and inadequate food and water supplies" (ROOTS 1988, 5).

An Israeli soldier, Dr. Portnoy, described Ansar as "a concentration camp not fit for animals to live in." Ansar II was opened in 1986 in Gaza. It mainly contained Palestinian boys aged 13 to 20 from Gaza, who had been rounded up in mass raids and imprisoned for varying periods as a means of collective punishment. In its special report on Ansar II, the Data Base Project described the harsh conditions experienced by these youths: "armed soldiers guarding 24 hours per day inside and the door kept open. Prisoners could not walk, talk to one another or eat without permission." Army surveillance was persistent. Prisoners "could not wash or even take a drink of water. They were taken only once a day to the outside toilets—holes dug in the open sand—where they were watched under gunpoint" (ROOTS 1988, 5–6).

Environmental Conditions

Although it shared some of the brutal characteristics of Ansar I and Ansar II, Ansar III remains the worse in terms of its conditions due to its environment. It is one of the largest Israeli prisons today (Habash 2019). The Roots and Friends of Palestinian Prisoners report outlines how Israeli restrictions make the prisoners' lives even harder. These restrictions include refusing to allow prisoners to "lower the flaps of their tents during the day, not permitting them to cover their heads during the count while they sit under the intense desert sun or not allowing them to remove their shirts, restricting the use of water, bathrooms and showers" which "border on the sadistic" (1988, 7). According to Tamar Pelleg, an Israeli attorney from the Association for Civil Rights who visited Ansar III in 1988, the prison is "a barbed wire enclosure, within which tents have been planted in endless rows."

> The tents, one almost on top of the other, are filled to overflow with detainees, who spend their days stretched out on their wooden bunks. The only piece of greenery that meets the eye is in the vicinity of prison headquarters. The detainees, who have lost all semblance of individual identity, are kept incommunicado from the outside world, and in enforced idleness. They are cut off from everything but the here and now. (ROOTS 1988, 7)

Collective Punishment

Collective punishment, abuse, and humiliation were important in Ansar III and remain so today. Tamar Pelleg reports that "prisoners had to get down on their knees, lower their heads and remain in that position all through the cold night. Anyone raising his head was cursed and beaten." Furthermore:

> Even the daily head counts are used as occasions for humiliation by the guards. The practice in itself is merely designed as a humiliation, since escape from Ansar III into the desert is unlikely. Counting takes place three times a day and can drag on for more than an hour as each is compelled to undergo a ritual of jumping up, turning around and calling out his number. The other prisoners must wait under the desert sun until the entire process is completed. Frequently, guards extend the counting period and search the tents and destroy the meager possessions of the prisoners. It is not uncommon for detainees to faint from sunstroke during the noonday count. (ROOTS 1988, 10)

Following a visit on 2 June 1988, one of the few western journalists allowed to visit Ansar III was Glenn Frankel of *the Washington Post*, who revealed that an "Israeli reservist who did not give his name, sought out this correspondent during today's visit and alleged that beatings occurred regularly."

> *"If someone talks back or has his shirt unbuttoned, they will hit you," said the guard, who said he had been serving at the camp for nearly two weeks. They take them into the shower room and beat them, not with instruments but with their hands and feet. It is just done out of sadism—people are bored.* (ROOTS 1988, 11)

Such beatings are not only arbitrary but also common among guards who "are encouraged by the example set by the Israeli camp commander himself," who was witnessed beating prisoners. During a clash, "the commander Col. Tsemach pulled out his pistol and shot a prisoner to death at close range" (ROOTS 1988, 11). Today, forms of torture may be more psychologically focused, but, as the literature and prisoners interviewed for this work teach us, it can be even more severe and humiliating.

Solitary Confinement

One of the most frequently used methods of punishment continues to be solitary confinement. In the 1980s, the solitary cell was more of "a prefabricated corrugated metal box, similar to a standup coffin, which has the effect of becoming like a toaster oven under the intense desert sun." In the words of the human rights organization al-Haq, "The *zinzanis* (cells) are small and unbearably hot and smell from uncleared excrement. The prisoners are handcuffed or bound hand and foot during the time they are in isolation" (ROOTS 1988, 11). This is in addition to crowded cells that are only two square meters. At times, 20 people are crammed there at once (ROOTS 1988, 11).

Solitary confinement continues to be used in Ansar III and other Israeli prisons. It is one of the main reasons why prisoners embark on hunger strikes. In 2017, Palestinian prisoners organized a massive hunger strike to denounce some prison policies and to demand an end to solitary confinement—especially long-term isolation for security reasons. However, as of this writing, the Israeli Prison Services continues to use isolation against Palestinians, with tens of thousands of prisoners historically held in solitary confinement and isolation (Addameer n.d., d, 1).

Banning Communication

Hunger strikes work best when "bystanders and third parties are mobilized to join in" (Khazan 2013). To prevent such mobilization, Israeli prison authorities attempt to ban the communication of prisoners with the outside world. This has been the case in remote prisons, like Nafha, and in prisons less remote in the West Bank. In other prison contexts, limiting, and at times, banning communication is important for authorities to ensure less mobilization and solidarity actions.

In this context, the Obama administration calculated that the American public at large was indifferent to the plight of Guantánamo inmates (Rosenthal 2013) and attempted to ban communication from Guantánamo. American prison authorities' attempts to ban communications flowing out of Guantánamo have limited the world's knowledge of hunger strike dynamics in the detention center. The US military command forbade prisoners from sending letters or updates and stopped releasing information about hunger strikes, after accusing the strikers of attempting to manipulate public opinion through false accusations—an accusation that the prisoners have always denied in their letters (McFadden 2013). It was also up to the Guantánamo attorneys and to journalists, then, to disobey the gag order, which was a significant personal risk for them to take on (Begg interview). These prison repression tactics are by no means limited to Guantánamo, since, as shown elsewhere in this monograph, prisoners must surmount significant barriers to communicate with the world outside through letters and phones.

Hunger Strikers' Response to Repression

Repression does not stop after hunger strikes end. It is necessary to push against narratives that depict hunger strikers as resilient actors able to stay steadfast, defiant, and strong regardless of the repression used against them. Like us all, prisoners are human beings who have moments of fragility. They will ensure such moments are not shared with the Israeli authorities who, as several hunger strikers interviewed shared, are eager to capitalize on these moments to further repress them. Hence, it is important for hunger strikers to ensure the message they send to the prison authorities is one of strength and resistance. This is clearly manifested in their mottos, which emphasize that their action to achieve their demands is at the risk of death. This requires patience and persistence on the path they choose. In the words of 32-year-old former prisoner Hasan Shawka, "A hunger strike is a victory or a martyrdom, a choice that is difficult for any prisoner to make, but its price is freedom."

Shawka recalled a hunger striker who was transferred to a prison hospital and tied to a bed, while deprived of basic needs and placed under increased psychological strain. He lost his eyesight for three days on the 46th day of his strike. The Israeli authorities tried to persuade him to take a medical supplement to restore his eyesight so that he would not lose it completely. On day 52, he began to suffer from liver and kidney pain, and he began to see a color similar to blood in his urine. Here, the prison administration tried to bring in the force-feeding committee. Shawka resisted by threatening to stop drinking water. For him, the only options were death or freedom. After 65 days, the Israeli authorities surrendered to his demands. His detention was extended for a short period, and he was then released (Al-Assa 2019). Shawka's story, told from the point of view of hunger strikers, shows us the importance of sticking rigorously to the strike in the face of prison authorities' repression. Negotiation while on a hunger strike is in itself a political process that should be undertaken from a position of power. It has its own techniques, unpacked further in the next chapter.

Chapter 5. Negotiating During Hunger Strikes

This chapter focuses on the negotiation process between Palestinian hunger strikers and Israeli prison authorities, including how it starts and what leverage hunger strikers have within the prison context. It explores the role of intervention by political leaders from outside the prison on the course of negotiations, and it argues that, in contrast to public solidarity, these interventions have a largely negative impact on these processes. It also reveals the challenges that arise in prisoners' negotiations with prison authorities. In the words of former prisoner and hunger striker Fouad al-Qafash (2014):

> *A hunger strike is like a game. Who is going to surrender first, the prison or the prisoners? The ones dressed in military uniforms and armed with batons? Or the Palestinian prisoners who only have a strong will and faith in their cause?*

The word "negotiation" is itself contentious in the Palestinian context. It is often linked to so-called peace negotiations between the Palestinian Authority and the Israeli government, which have always led to further failures and setbacks for the Palestinians and further expansion of lands and resources for the Israelis. Hence, the word itself has become a perpetual dimension of Palestinian daily reality, with Palestinians often criticizing the PA leadership and its many attempts at failing the people in these negotiations. Drawing on prison imagery, Palestinian poet and human rights activist Rafeef Ziadah (2016) summarizes this well:

> *The Palestine I know does not care about a VIP pass*
> *She does not negotiate the size of our prison*
> *She does not negotiate the size of our prison*
> *She breaks the walls*
> *She does not dialog across the bars*
> *She does not dialog across our prison bars*
> *She breaks those bars and beats them to the rhythm of old slave songs*
> *Freedom*
> *She breaks those bars and beats them to the rhythm of old slave songs*
> *Freedom*
> *She beats those bars,*
> *Beats those bars to the rhythm of old slave songs*
> *Freedom*
> *Freedom*
> *Freedom*

As Ziadah intuits, Palestinian prisoners recognize that negotiation with the Israeli state is futile unless it can be done from a position of power. That power is harnessed through hunger strikes, in which prisoners seize on the two areas in which they have leverage over their jailers: their bodies, and potential public support. At the same time, the prison authorities choose how and when to negotiate. They decide on the type of information allowed outside the prison, which can impact the support they receive. Even within the prison cell, prison medical staff can exaggerate the hunger strikers' illness and symptoms to push them to end their strike. In the words of Mithal Nassar (2014), a member of the Physicians for Human Rights–Israel's (PHRI) ethical committee, "The prison physician is not just a doctor. He is a military prison guard as well."

Ending a strike poses more challenges than starting one. The majority of hunger strikes end without an external party intervening. In a few recorded instances, the Palestinian Authority's intervention ended hunger strikes. In 1992, for example, Yasser Arafat, then chairman of the PLO, intervened to end a hunger strike (Genem interview). Israeli authorities permitted him to communicate with prisoners' leaders to negotiate an end to the strike. This instance of intervention by the PLO is a unique case not documented at any other time. However, such third-party interventions have been documented in other global contexts, including Northern Ireland. According to former IRA hunger striker Brendan McFarlane (2014), the IRA army council intervened in a popular 1981 hunger strike to question whether they actually thought about the consequences of their actions.

> [The] IRA army council on the outside sent them (the prisoners) individually a note. Very small, very short, and very hard. Comrade have you thought of the consequences of your decision. Do you realise that in three months you will be dead? And have you considered your family... so then the decision has to be, can I do this?

As for the 1992 Palestinian strike, it took place before the Oslo Process, and the PLO leadership was under the impression that the Israeli government would free prisoners if they ended the strike. Decades later, Israeli prisons still hold 26 prisoners who were imprisoned prior to Oslo and who had been encouraged to hope for release soon after the Oslo Agreement was signed in 1993.

Although the prisoners who were part of the 1992 hunger strike did not receive any promises that their demands would be met, several prisoners agreed to pause their strike. The prisoners in two striking prisons, Neve Tirza and Nafha, were an exception. The fact that Neve Tirza is a women's prison might help account for the different path the prisoners followed there, since, as noted above, female prisoners are generally more effective than men at organizing their actions and achieving their demands.

The majority of hunger strikes end as a result of internal intervention, when, in the view of the strike leaders, the strikes' demands have been or will be achieved. Hunger strikes that end without the leaders' approval often do not secure lasting changes for the prisoners, a point that further underscores the need for strong and effective leadership during a strike. Likewise, leaders who reject external intervention and rely on internal consensus tend to be more capable of achieving their demands. In the words of Suaad Genem, "prison hunger strikers who rejected the external intervention by Yasser Arafat achieved all of their demands. It just cost them one more day of striking, before the Israeli authorities invited the strike leader for a meeting to negotiate their demands." For Genem, the negotiation process requires patience. Sometimes, just one day or a few hours is required. On other occasions, it takes much longer to get the Israeli authorities to sit down and give in to the hunger strikers' demands.

Even when a strike ends, it can be relaunched. In previous negotiations, the Israeli authorities have agreed to the hunger strikers' demands, only to break their promises once the hunger strikers end their action. In an interview, hunger striker Anas Abu Khudair[14] explained this process in detail. Abu Khudair was detained by Israeli authorities, who accused him of planning to "capture an Israeli soldier for an exchange deal" to secure the release of Palestinian political prisoners. He was sentenced to 39 months in prison. Abu Khudair explained that, in many cases, "the IPS conceded to prisoners' demands, or to some of them, so that prisoners would end their hunger strike. However, promises were broken. [This happened to] Abdullah Abu Jaber, who went for a 24-day hunger strike, and to Ala Hammad." The prisoners either ended their strike with nothing achieved or they achieved some or all of their demands but later had those gains reversed.

Hunger strikers often fear that what they achieve through negotiations with the IPS will eventually be taken away by the same authorities. This "concede and renege" approach is part of the psychological warfare that the Israeli state uses to persuade prisoners that their strikes are futile. This is done to discourage potential future hunger strikes. In the prisoners' letters to the IPS, they often demand "serious negotiations" that will ensure that the authorities will not renege. In 2017, Karim Younis, one of the leaders of the hunger strike that year and the longest-serving Palestinian prisoner (he was arrested in 1983 and is serving a sentence due to end in 2023), wrote to the IPS administration that the prisoners were "only ready for serious negotiations, not for meaningless sessions or empty promises" (ICSFT 2017). Negotiations that are not carried out in good faith are frustrating for prisoners and their supporters. Prisoners become wary of promises that are easily broken and negotiation sessions that achieve nothing other than distracting them from their demands. For hunger strikers, a negotiation process is considered fruitful if it is swiftly followed by the implementation of the

---

14   Abu Khudair was arrested in 20016 in Hebron in the West Bank where he traveled to attend his sister's wedding.

strikers' demands and if the promises made by the authorities during negotiations are honored. Successful implementation also depends on the strength and firmness of the prisoners' leadership, and whether they are willing to compromise on nonessential demands in order to enable negotiations to continue.

The next chapter addresses the contentious question of what makes hunger strikes successful. It asks whether success is best measured by whether the demands were achieved or whether it should instead be considered in broader terms. Before addressing that topic, we must examine a wide range of cases involving both male and female Palestinian political prisoners to better understand Palestinians' personal experience of hunger strikes and to see how they view such practices through a gender-attentive lens.

Chapter 6. The Efficacy of Hunger Strikes

This chapter addresses what it means to claim success in a hunger strike. It also examines a 2004 hunger strike in Israeli prisons, which was identified as a key historical moment for many prisoners. It analyzes the lessons learned from this strike, using the words of those who were part of it. As one Palestinian prisoner put it:

> *Everything inside the prison has a story of resistance behind it. So, as I said, is everything you find in prison, the blanket, the cup, the pens, the paper, the books in the library, the food. There is a story of the struggle behind this. And one day it was one of the prisoners' demands in their hunger strikes.* (Norman 2021, 84)

It is by prison resistance—most significantly hunger strikes—that prisoners achieved these demands. In this chapter, we discuss several other examples of such achievements, including ending the forced use of *"ya sidi"* ("my lord") in Israeli prisons. We refer to success in a situation when hunger strikers' demands were met. We use the term "efficacy" to describe the larger impacts of hunger strikes, which range from raising awareness to promoting solidarity actions that transformed Israeli policies to the benefit of Palestinian prisoners and hunger strikers.

Until the twenty-first century, most Palestinian hunger strikes were collective protests involving many prisoners and various prison facilities simultaneously. These strikes established prisoners' committees and standard negotiating procedures. The strikes were disrupted by the authorities who isolated leaders in solitary confinement, preventing communication between prisoners and severing their contacts with the outside world.

Similar patterns can be discerned elsewhere: the prisons of Northern Ireland and South Africa offered favorable environments for collective hunger strikes. Although they were not always successful in the short term, over the long term the anti-apartheid movement and the movement for an independent Ireland did achieve some of their aims, including the legal end of apartheid in South Africa and constitutional representation in Ireland. While prisoners were released as a result of internationally brokered agreements—including the Oslo Accords, the Good Friday Agreement, and the negotiations to end apartheid in South Africa—some of the gains from these collective actions diminished over time. A more recent and common pattern has seen individual hunger strikes undertaken mainly in the hope of securing release from prison.

In practice, wherever prison authorities give in to prisoners' demands, the same authorities typically reverse such agreements at a later date. However, protest actions, collective and individual, continue because they expose the inhumane conditions of the imprisonment and attract support from foreign organizations. These dynamics are crucial to the wider project of liberation.

While the interviews conducted for this research show that success is not easily defined, one basic aspect of success that interviewees repeatedly referred to was achieving their demands. However, what constitutes success for one individual may not be success for others. We see it clearly in the case of Hana Shalabi, who asked for her freedom—a demand that she achieved following 55 days of hunger striking. However, she was deported to the Gaza Strip, away from her hometown of Jenin. Shalabi remains stuck in Gaza, unable to return to and reunite with her family. While her freedom may be termed a success, it would be more precise to say that it was a temporary success, since the Israeli authorities rescinded their promise and did not permit her to join her family.

Some hunger strikes achieved none of their demands: should these be regarded as failures? These questions cannot be answered in a straightforward manner due to the complexities surrounding the declaration of demands. The hunger strikers interviewed for this research emphasized that there are always demands for which success cannot be measured, such as maintaining what they called "lasting outcomes." Such outcomes are not always visible at the time of the hunger strike itself, due to the lack of precise communication among strikers that results from their being held in solitary confinement, and because they lack access to lawyers and visits from family members.

Success, on the other hand, can also relate to visibility, the impact on the wider community, and the enduring results of hunger strikers' demands. Related to visibility is the work of lawyers and the supporting community in visualizing hunger strikers' condition to the outside world through pictures, videos, and letters. Several pictures were taken of Samer Issawi during his hunger strike. One picture from February 19, 2013, shows Issawi next to three Israeli prison officers as he leaves Jerusalem's magistrate court. Issawi, with his emaciated body, sat in a wheelchair next to three strong police officers. Issawi's face shows strength and courage while raising his hands with the V sign (used as a gesture of victory) while the Israeli officers' faces are absent. Such pictures are often shared widely on social media and encourage further support and solidarity with hunger strikers (Awwad in Kuttab 2013).

Also related to visibility is the ability to create an atmosphere of unity around the decision to strike. The demand itself is a revolutionary act. Embarking on a hunger strike to undermine oppressors and to articulate clear demands transforms an act of seeming desperation, undertaken as a last resort, into an intentional act, distinguishing it from other self-sacrificial acts that involve the weaponization of life, such as suicide. Even hunger strikes that end in the strikers' death are distinct from suicide: they assert the prisoners' will against the dehumanization of imprisonment. Generally, they are undertaken for the sake of a cause, rather than simply for the striker's personal benefit. In this regard, prison hunger strikes resemble martyrdom—even when they are not necessarily fatal—more than suicide. In Palestine, martyrdom resonates profoundly with both religious and nonreligious communities.

The visibility of hunger strikers' demands figures significantly into their efficacy, which cannot be measured in purely quantitative terms of success and failure. A hunger strike may start and finish without the prisoners' demands achieving adequate visibility either inside or outside the prison, thus raising no awareness of the conditions of imprisonment. As a result, the solidarity of action that characterizes any impactful hunger strike, which is crucial in exposing any injustice and achieving demands, is absent.

Actions that spread transnational and domestic awareness about hunger strikes are essential, even if there is no clear or short-term outcome. This is maintained through several means, including the emotive impact on the local (and even global) community keeping the pressure on the authorities to permanently agree to the prisoners' demands. Here too, efficacy is measured in more than quantitative terms; it refers to an attitude, and a state of mind, that instills resilience

Visibility means more than simply achieving immediate demands.

and a sense of purpose in a resistance struggle. In all the cases of prison hunger strikes discussed in this monograph, awareness and experiential aspects of the demands of earlier hunger strikes in previous decades substantively influenced later actions and impacted their long-term efficacy.

As a rubric for measuring success, visibility means more than simply achieving immediate demands. From this vantage point, the measurement of whether the demands were achieved comes to appear as simplistic and excessively utilitarian. To the extent that any analysis of success is limited to measuring outcomes, visibility is ignored, as is the value of consciousness-raising, in general. The interviews with hunger strikers that have formed the substance of this monograph demonstrate that prisoners themselves care not only about immediate responses by prison authorities but also about the long-term efficacy of those outcomes.

Placing these different dimensions into perspective and considering the demands of hunger strikes outlined in this monograph—from improving prison conditions and providing educational opportunities, to demanding freedom—makes it clear that none of the hunger strikes discussed can be defined as a complete failure: at the very least, they all have raised awareness about the conditions of imprisonment. And even when none of the demands are achieved, the decision to embark on a potentially fatal action instigates a wide range of solidarity actions: protests, petitions to relevant authorities, and social media campaigns that create solidarity across the community. Each of these has the potential to change the conditions of imprisonment.

There are also successful hunger strikes, such as the ones calling for an end to forced prison labor or the use of humiliating words such as "*ya sidi*" in Israeli prisons. The term is dehumanizing because it equates prisoners with slaves and jailers with lords. Both tactics of forced labor and dehumanizing words are no longer used in Israeli prisons, and they seem to have not been brought back. Prisoners described how the term *ya sidi* was removed from the prison lexicon:

> *On July 8, 1970, the fourth day of the hunger strike, the prison officer entered one prison's section, and asked, "what do you want?" We responded by stating our needs. He then asked why you are not using the word "My lord"? We replied that the time for that is over and will never come back....* (Abu Ghoush, Adnan, and Abu Baker 2004)

The term *ya sidi* is no longer used in Israeli prisons, thanks to these prisoners' hunger strikes. It was important that the prison administration realized that dignity (*karama)* has a high cost that prisoners are not willing to surrender.

At the same time, several Palestinian hunger strikes that called for an end to administrative detention cannot be said to be completely or permanently successful, even if they were effective in the short term. Occasionally, all the strikers' demands were met by the Israeli authorities, but these successes were short-lived. They did not bring positive change in prison conditions over the long term. Instead, they led to mounting suppression against the prisoners involved. The same patterns can be observed in the cases of Guantánamo Detention Center and Iranian prisons—temporary concessions were often withdrawn soon after hunger strikes were concluded.

These metrics of success and effectiveness in hunger strikes are not absolute. Rather, they are organic attempts to measure the outcomes[15] and wider impacts[16] of hunger strikes. Such difficulties and uncertainties characterize other resistance methods, such as protests and boycott actions, which also present a challenge to traditional quantitative measurements of success. Achieving no demands does not necessarily equal failure. Deciding to embark on a hunger strike that can easily damage one's health is a courageous decision that cannot be readily associated with a failure. Moreover, the contribution that hunger strikers make to broaden the collective awareness of the injustices they face more than justifies this form of political resistance. Raising global awareness concerning prison conditions figures crucially

---

15   Outcomes here refers to direct results for the hunger strikers themselves—that is, success.

16   Wider impacts here refers to those that concern the wider Prisoners Movement: the effectiveness for all prisoners.

How the cells of Palestinian prisoners changed with hunger strikes

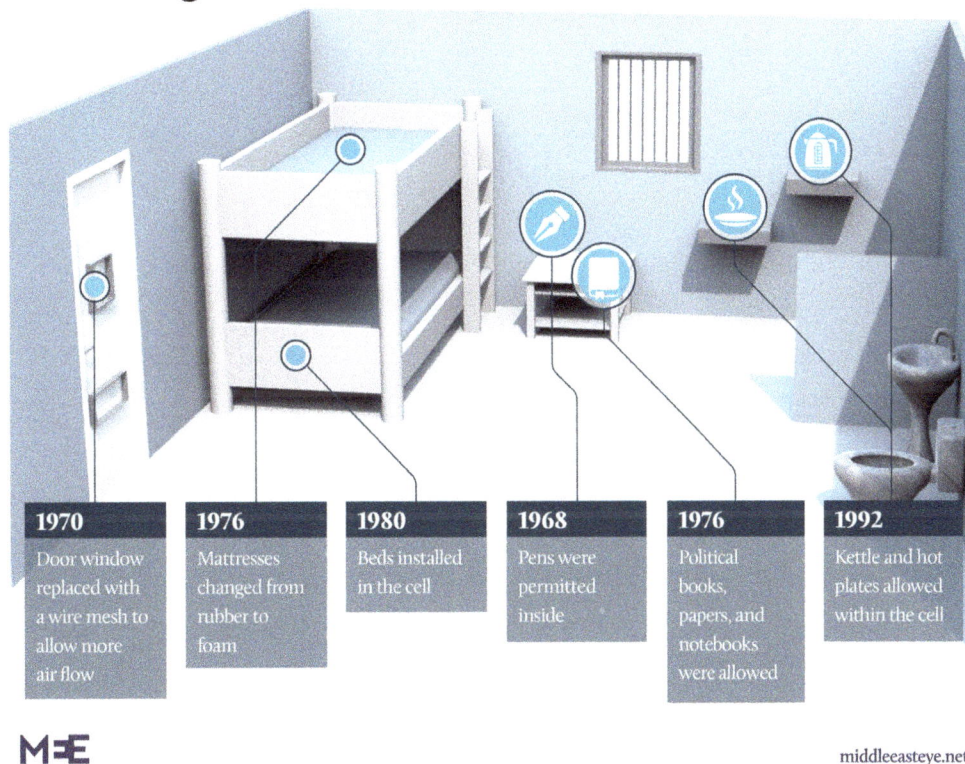

1970	1976	1980	1968	1976	1992
Door window replaced with a wire mesh to allow more air flow	Mattresses changed from rubber to foam	Beds installed in the cell	Pens were permitted inside	Political books, papers, and notebooks were allowed	Kettle and hot plates allowed within the cell

M≡E

middleeasteye.net

FIGURE 4: A FEW CHANGES IN ISRAELI PRISON CELLS AS A RESULT OF PALESTINIAN HUNGER STRIKES

Source: Abu Sneineh 2019

into the logic, dynamics, and motivations underwriting hunger strikes. None of this, however, detracts from the emotional devastation that prisoners may experience following a hunger strike that achieved none of their demands, especially since such outcomes make it easier for prison authorities to mock and divide prisoners, after they have sacrificed their health and risked their lives while appearing to have achieved nothing (Malasa and Badran interviews).

Figure 4 is an example of how Israeli prison cells changed as a result of Palestinian hunger strikes between 1970 and 1992, showing a clear improvement, including the change from mattresses to rubber foam in 1976, and the installation of beds in the prison cells in 1980.

Efficacy of Hunger Strikes During the Post-Oslo Prisoners' Movement

The Palestinian prisoners' movement changed in the post-Oslo period, from 1993 onwards. The once-robust Palestinian prisoners' movement is no longer as unified, and there is a growing division between Hamas and Fatah. These political divisions have fragmented solidarity among prisoners, affecting the amount of support hunger strikers receive, especially from these divided parties. Such divisions are Palestinian prisoners' "biggest problem," according to Khader Adnan. The tendency to weaponize life through hunger strikes indicates a loss of confidence and trust in existing political structures (including political parties) and their ability to address the prisoners' demands. This division is "reproduced behind bars and manifested in the lack of collective actions" by prisoners. This leaves prisoners with "no other option but to decide to go on hunger strike on their own," Adnan adds (Hassan 2016). Israeli prison authorities have capitalized on this climate to divide prisoners.

The appointment and policies of IPS Commissioner Ya'acov Ganot further exacerbated divisions among the prisoners. Ganot's appointment as head of the IPS (2003–2007) coincided with prisoners' growing loss of trust in the PA's leadership and its ability to release all prisoners. Ganot received direct support from then–Prime Minister Ariel Sharon, who was his former commanding officer in Paratroopers Battalion 101 (Dakka 2009; Abu Atwan interview). This allowed him to overcome bureaucratic and administrative obstacles that would normally have stood in the way of his restructuring prison administration.[17] Sharon gave him a free hand to apply new policies. He even increased Ganot's budget so that the old prisons could be equipped with new technology and systems that would simplify the monitoring and surveillance of prisoners, and require less human intervention (Dakka 2009).

Ganot began antagonizing prisoners as soon as he took up his new position. In 2003, prisoners were attacked with gas and batons in Askalan Prison (Ashkelon), leading to several injuries. It is unclear whether these attacks were in response to any prior provocation. Legislation was introduced to mandate strip searches and glass barriers in visiting rooms so that prisoners were completely physically separated from family (Safadi, Hamad, and Malasa interviews). These barriers have the effect of dividing prisoners from each other: now they are placed between the prisoners and their families, making physical contact impossible, unless the Israeli prison authorities allow it. The barriers also limit prisoners' communication with visitors, mostly immediate family members. Communications become limited to speaking to the glass barrier behind which the prisoner sits. Convening awareness sessions in which

---

17   IPS policies changed under Ganot not only due to his leadership but also because of Sharon's political influence at that time, the Second Intifada, and the fact that many prisons around the world were introducing similar surveillance mechanisms, including Guantánamo, which influenced Israeli surveillance policies (Abu Atwan, al-Faleet, Begg, and Norman interviews).

prisoners can discuss politics and coordinating collectively becomes harder. As a result, new and inexperienced prisoners are left untrained.

Israeli authorities seized on this political division and fragmentation among Palestinian prisoners, driving prisoners to embark on hunger strikes. Why would the Israeli authorities want prisoners to go on a hunger strike? Embarking on a strike while divided can be counterproductive and demoralizing for prisoners. There is a higher chance of them failing to achieve demands and also of achievements from previous hunger strikes being withdrawn. Such outcomes are discouraging for prisoners and further increase their infighting as well as their sense of passivity.

This is exactly what happened in 2004. Three of the political prisoners interviewed for this research—Fouad al-Qafash, Ayman al-Sharawna, and Mazin Malasa—recollected this dynamic in different yet overlapping ways:

> *The IPS always tried to break the strike. After three weeks of starvation, the strikers felt depressed and defeated. This was what stopped them from going on hunger strike between 2004 and 2012. When a strike fails, prisoners lose hope.* (Al-Qafash interview)

> *Some 19 days after the hunger strike, prisoners failed to get their demands met. We were defeated. The prisoners' spirits were crushed. I saw many of them crying. About 9,000 of them endured 19 days of hunger strike but achieved nothing.* (Al-Sharawna interview)

> *This was a win for the authorities and the prisoners lost. We ended up in a hard situation. I have never shared this feeling with anyone before. Due to this failure, our situation prior to the strike was much better than after the strike. We learned from our mistakes. We see where our mistakes are. It is important to keep trying. A failed attempt is a good way to [eventually] succeed.* (Malasa interview)

Israeli authorities used these setbacks to disavow their earlier concessions to the prisoners' movement during the preceding 35 years (1968–2003). These concessions had been accomplished through several open hunger strikes in which six prisoners died hunger striking. Many of these were force-fed, as elaborated in Chapter 4. One of these victims was Hussein Obeidat, who lost his life in Askalan prison in 1992 while participating in the general hunger strike of all prisons (Abu Arafeh 2017, 321; Farwana 2017).

The withdrawal of concessions demoralized the hunger strikers. Such outcomes might deter prisoners from joining further hunger strikes. But that is not always the case. The interviews used in this monograph show clearly that hunger strikers often bounce back and resist the withdrawal of concessions, if not through further hunger strikes, then through other means of resistance. Our research suggests that hunger strikes are still relatively successful and effective when one considers all instances, ranging from cases where all demands were met to ones in which no demands were achieved. To put the matter of success into context, this chapter's concluding section examines the 2004 Palestinian hunger strike and considers how it impacts the prisoners' movement to this day.

The 2004 Palestinian Hunger Strike

For prisoners contemplating hunger strikes to advance their struggle for justice and freedom, unity is key—among themselves as well as with the wider community outside prison walls. In the Palestinian case, the depth of the crisis exemplified by the hunger strike of 2004 impeded prisoners from returning to their former practice of collective hunger strikes. This was the first hunger strike in which prisoners achieved none of their demands. The strike of 2004 is probably the least successful hunger strike in Palestinian history (Al-Sharawna 2014). Prison conditions took a turn for the worse. The treatment of prisoners was especially affected. Even when Ganot left his position at the IPS in 2007 and became Israel's General Manager of the Airports Authority, his policies remained in place. Prisoners' inability to fight collectively became "inherited," as Dakka (2009) termed it. Before 2004, the IPS director was "terrified when he visited the prison," but he later "ignored prisoners' representatives and acted arrogantly" (Al-Sharawna 2014).

The decision to embark on further strikes following the failure of 2004 was a difficult one. Prisoners feared another defeat. At the same time, they were desperate. This desperation was shared by many families who were banned from visits for years. Prisoner Abdullah Barghouti, for example, was banned for ten years from having family visits (Al-Qafash 2014). This desperation was shared by prisoners in solitary confinement. In 2012, the increasingly poor conditions of the prisoners were part of the political opportunity structure that was needed to motivate the protest. Prisoners were the resource, with their own agency, for initiating the action. They were ready to go as far as death to improve their prison conditions.

Having the right political time or the necessary resources are not absolute determinants of whether collective action will occur (Scanlan, et al. 2008, 307). Emotions and personal agency are equally important. Testimonies of prisoners interviewed for this research show that the years of uncertainty, poor treatment, and the mounting emotions of the prisoners and their families weighed heavily on them. They were mentally exhausted. The interviews conducted for this research also show how emotions energize collective protest and stimulate the larger social movement. Fear and anger are needed to mobilize and to cement cohesiveness between prisoners and the outside community. Emotions of this sort are vital for motivating and sustaining protest and for making a long-term impact.

Generally, all Palestinian hunger strikes are associated with slogans centered around dignity (*karama*). For example, in 2012 and 2014, we hear many slogans and phrases raised by hunger strikes, including "The strike of freedom and dignity [*idrab al-huriyya wa al-karama*]," which highlighted prisoners' refusal to submit to an existence without dignity. Such slogans aligned with the concepts of protest suicide (Andriolo 2006) and revolutionary suicide (Newton 1973). Both Andriolo and Newton refer to rational and deliberate acts of self-sacrifice to confront injustice, and they distinguish these from suicide as a goal in itself. Such self-sacrifice is seen as far preferable to enduring the wrongs imposed on the protester (Scanlan, et al. 2008, 281). Prisoners "love the concept of a free life" and thus "do not hesitate to risk their own lives" to "seek a decent and free life for their people," ex-prisoner and Palestinian writer Ahmed Qattamesh wrote in 1982. Qattamesh added: "A life of humiliation that is subject to restrictions, oppression, and exploitation is not free"; it is rather "A miserable existence that needs to be changed" (Fanon 1982, 5). Qattamesh articulates with these words prisoners' motivation to weaponize their own lives, using necroresistance.

Prisoners are able to use the moral outrage associated with the deteriorating prison conditions to advance their cause. They are also able to capitalize on their families' longing to visit them. Both hold a vital place in the sympathy and solidarity that strikes generate. The unity generated by the 28-day hunger strike in 2012 was remarkable. Some 2,000 prisoners, from all political parties and the majority of Israeli prisons, were ready to lose their lives to be treated with dignity (Sherwood 2012; Mashharawi 2014).[18] They were ready to push the Israeli authorities to allow family visits from Gaza after seven years of bans (Al-Sharawna 2014), following the capture of Shalit. They also wanted to free inmates from solitary confinement, as one prisoner recollected:

> *I know what solitary confinement means.... Abdullah Barghouti was prevented from seeing his family for 10 years. The Supreme Court only allowed him to see his little girl from behind a glass window without the right to speak to her.... The prisoners... put up with pain and hunger for 28 days just to get him freed.... They were willing to risk their own lives so that their fellow prisoner could see his little girl.* (Al-Qafash 2014)

In the interlocutors' own words, prisoners succeeded and had their demands met. Al-Sharawna commented, "We achieved an unprecedented victory" (2014). When the strike concluded, chief hunger striker Othman Saeed Bilal announced to all prisoners, "We have won. You can now eat." Bilal told them, "No prisoner will have to live in solitary from now on.

---

18   Notwithstanding its unity, this was not a collective hunger strike per se but rather a semi-collective one. According to Addameer statistics (April 2012), there were 4,410 prisoners at the time of the strike. The percentage of prisoners involved in the strike was less than half of the prisoner population. Thus, the strike of 2012 should not be classified as a collective hunger strike (involving the majority of prisoners) or a general hunger strike (involving all prisoners), but rather as a semi-collective strike.

Today, you have beaten the prison service. We have freed everyone in solitary confinement" (Al-Qafash 2014).

Bilal and al-Sharawna's words show the importance of hunger strike leaders—in this case, Othman Bilal—in ending the strike. Prisoners will only end their strikes when the leader tells them to do so. This ensures that Israeli prison authorities cannot manipulate or control the narrative around when a strike ends, especially when different prisons are taking part. It also shows how hunger strikes are acts of collective solidarity with those who live in far more confining conditions—in this case, those in solitary confinement. A successful hunger strike does much more than achieve the strike's demands; it also makes a long-term impact on the prisoners' conditions. In the 2012 hunger strike, freeing prisoners from solitary confinement was another collective success for hunger strikers.

Lessons and Takeaways

In this final chapter, we identify key lessons from more successful hunger strikes that are relevant to outside sympathizers as well as to prisoners who either embark on or plan hunger strikes. We then outline actionable takeaways of this research for sympathizers on one hand and activists and practitioners on the other.

Three Lessons for the Public: Resistance, Solidarity, and the Social Context

The first key lesson of our research and interviews is that even in the most restricted and inhuman prison spaces resistance can flourish. The hunger strikers interviewed for this research consistently emphasized that hunger strikes are a last resort after all other mechanisms of pressure on the prison authorities—including negotiations and protest—have been exhausted. Even though the key strategic goal of hunger strikers is not to die but to achieve practical demands, hunger strikers do prepare themselves to give their lives for the higher, moral goal of preserving their dignity. Though more often than not they survive the ordeal, the act of resistance in itself solidifies their resolution and often advances their general causes to stand up against oppression and defend their human dignity.

The second lesson drawn from our research on Palestinian hunger strikers is that solidarity plays a significant role in effective resistance. *Solidarity* should be conceived of as a verb. It is an action. It is neither performative nor passive. Solidarity means much more than social media posts or mere conversation. Active solidarity challenges colonial structures and power imbalances. It actively pushes for justice for the collective on the ground. If solidarity does not challenge those dynamics, it is passive. Passive solidarity comes from a position of power. It ensures that passive supporters and their audience remain comfortable with their positions of privilege. Privileged as they are in this power imbalance, they choose to stay neutral or offer performative statements that do not get at the root causes of violence in Palestine—which is a perpetually violent settler-colonial project. In this context, any solidarity that does not actively stop the constant violations of human rights in Palestine and push for accountability is passive. Palestinian hunger strikers need active—not passive—solidarity from their sympathizers and allies.

The third and final lesson is that, even when they embark on a strike while in solitary confinement, hunger strikers never act alone. Even individual hunger strikes are collective in the sense that their strikes are often undertaken to improve the shared conditions of all the prisoners. Every hunger strike is also collective—or rather, collaborative—in that every hunger strike presupposes an audience. Hunger strikes are always announced, whether through open letters that circulate widely or through discreet communication networks inside and outside prisons. Prisoners often target specific audiences and hope that the media coverage and public support for their strikes will widen the circle of observers. Hunger strikes are never random acts and they cannot be solipsistic. Hunger strikers who die do so for a collective cause, not, as Ian Miller states concerning Northern Ireland, to "selfishly escape individual suffering or institutional misery. Their deaths were altruistic, selfless, acts performed for the greater good of a national cause" (2016, 2).

Takeaways for Sympathizers and Allies

Our research has identified actionable takeaways for sympathizers and allies in three distinct yet related domains: solidarity actions, engagement with the media, and using the "political prisoner" designation.

Join or Organize Popular Solidarity Campaigns

Whether using public demonstrations, letter-writing campaigns, sit-ins, protests, or social media campaigns, solidarity organizations and individuals can use a wide range of solidarity actions to raise the visibility of prison hunger strikes for the wider public.

Popular protests, sit-ins, and demonstrations in solidarity with hunger strikers that take place outside prisons put pressure on prison authorities and their superiors to give in to the strikers' demands. Even solidarity actions that occur geographically farther away from the prison can pressure local and central governments to submit to their demands. In Palestine, we see this clearly in popular protests that have taken place in Palestinian cities, often led by prisoners' families and garnering coverage from the news media. All this contributed to the success of the 2012 hunger strikes (Mashharawi 2014; Sarsak 2016).

In addition to protesting outside prisons and in city centers, allies can use the digital space to increase the visibility of prison hunger strikes. Social media presence is a crucial tool for increasing visibility. Twitter occupies an important domain for expressions of support for Palestinian prison hunger strikers and has a greater impact on the course of prison hunger strikes across the Middle East than other platforms such as Facebook and Instagram.[19] These platforms have not been as popular among Palestinian activists —most probably due to content censorship. In September 2022, a new report, commissioned by Meta (which owns Facebook

---

19   As of this writing, prominent Twitter accounts that cover Palestinian hunger strikes include the Quds News Network (Arabic @qudsn; English @QudsNen) and @PalPrisoners. For Iranian prison hunger strikes, excellent coverage is provided by the Abdorrahman Boroumand Center (@IranRights_org) and Human Rights Activists in Iran (@hra_news).

and Instagram) and conducted by the independent consultancy Business for Social Responsibility, found that Meta censored Palestinian content on both social media platforms. The report concludes that Meta removed social media content that document Israeli human rights abuses during the May 2021 Israeli attack on Gaza (Biddle 2022). This censorship harms human rights, in a world where social media allows activists and their allies to shape directly the narrative of the prison hunger strike by bringing attention to the needs of the prisoners, their strikes, and solidarity actions outside the prisons.

Engage the Media

A second takeaway for allies is that they must engage with news media as a part of their support for hunger strikers. Media has a crucial role in increasing public support for hunger strikers and in raising the visibility of solidarity actions. Traditional news media coverage of the hunger strike can affect its outcome. It has a positive effect when it expands support from the public, including both sympathizers and neutral bystanders. And it has a negative effect when it fails to grow sympathy for and awareness of the strikers. Palestinian hunger strikers emphasized the significance of fair news coverage and balanced reporting about their anti-colonial struggle in both local and international media.

The media can also positively affect outcomes when providing coverage of the popular protests and solidarity actions that accompany the hunger strikes. Armed with the awareness of the extent to which media representations can be shaped by popular protests, the most impactful work that sympathetic activists can do is to engage with multiple media outlets at the local, regional, and international levels to ensure coverage of these solidarity actions.

A major challenge for hunger strikers is that access to mainstream media tends to be limited and biased. Interviewees noted that supportive media coverage reaches people who are already sympathetic to the Palestinian cause, and thereby preaches to the already converted, often failing to reach new people. Palestinian prisoners believe that their actions reported outside Palestine come with a pro-Israel bias. A different kind of media bias is at play in cases such as Guantánamo, in which the US media caters to a public that tends to look negatively on anyone alleged to be a combatant in the War on Terror (Khazan 2013). In the Iranian context, political prisoners who embark on hunger strikes are simply neglected and forgotten by the international media and the global public. Every carceral context presents a different kind of media bias, but in each case, such bias is a determining factor in whether a hunger strike will impact public awareness of the prisoners' struggles.

Thus, solidarity from sympathetic allies should be twofold. First, supporters should identify the venues and forums that are most likely to portray the hunger strikers' plight with fairness, and they should promote awareness through these sympathetic channels. In the Palestinian context, these would be venues like *Al Jazeera, Middle East Eye,* and *The Electronic Intifada.*

Second, it is crucial that sympathizers engage with mainstream media and seek to challenge any biases directly in order to have the widest possible impact.

Use the "Political Prisoner" Designation as Narrative
A third takeaway for allies and sympathizers who wish to support hunger-striking prisoners is that they should not allow authorities to determine who can and cannot legitimately be designated as political prisoners. This determination must be made by prisoners themselves rather than by prison authorities or by the state that incarcerates them. In Palestine, prisoners are incarcerated within the context of international geopolitics—particularly Israel's settler-colonial project—and are often imprisoned under the guise of state security. Minor and non-criminal offenses are elevated to the level of state security violations and used to incarcerate and thus subjugate Palestinians. The Israeli state does not admit to the political nature of imprisonments, though Palestinian prisoners self-identify themselves as political prisoners.

It is through the act of embarking on hunger strikes that prisoners establish their identity as political prisoners. Allies of prison hunger strikers must recognize this identity, and by embracing it, they will be in position to promote resisters' discourse. Prisoners' choices and self-determination must also be respected; extending such respect is a preliminary step for any strategically effective form of outside solidarity. Allies should use the political prisoner designation to inform the narrative that they promote in their protests, solidarity actions, and media campaigns. They should use their communications networks to help prisoners secure a wide acceptance of their self-identified status.

Takeaways for Hunger Strikers

Our research provides five takeaways for prison activists: how hunger strikers can effectively frame themselves, how they frame their actions to the public, how they time their strikes to mobilize incarcerated communities, how they prepare for strikes through awareness-raising sessions, and how they mitigate the health risks posed by the strike to themselves and others.

Frame Participants as Political Prisoners
Palestinian prisoners have won major concessions from prison authorities by embarking on hunger strikes despite seemingly insurmountable obstacles and adverse conditions. Palestinian hunger striker Mahmoud Sarsak recalled how he challenged the Israeli authorities over their definition of him as an "illegal combatant." He insisted that he was a political prisoner, held without charge or trial. This helped Sarsak—who later gained his freedom—because his

political imprisonment captured the attention of the international community. His case showed the importance of challenging Israeli discourse regarding how prisoners are defined.

Direct the Narrative Away from Self-Harm

Activists considering hunger strikes as part of their nonviolent struggle, whether from within prison or outside prison walls, might reflect on the extent to which a hunger strike is nonviolent when it leads to self-inflicted violence on the body and, in rare cases, to the striker's death. Here, Bargu's framing of the weaponization of life helps us adequately conceptualize hunger strikes; death is never a desired result. Nor is death—or any kind of self-harm—the ultimate purpose.

Hunger strikes are, first and foremost, tools of political resistance. Hunger strikers must reframe the narrative that their oppressors deploy—namely, that they are the primary cause of their own demise—and instead frame their suffering as a symptom of the oppression which they struggle against. The greater violence is the inhumane treatments that prison guards administer—such as force-feeding—under the guise of "helping" the strikers. Hunger strikers must frame their oppressors as the actor causing harm, and their own strike as an act of exercising their rights within the system that deprives them of most of their rights. By doing so, hunger strikers would more effectively make their case to the world.

Time Strikes to Maximize Mobilization

Another important takeaway for activists pertains to the timing of the hunger strike. Even strikes that may be perceived as unsuccessful—such as a strike that is not known beyond a small group of the strikers and their oppressors, or one that leads to no concessions from the target—can contribute to a rhythm of multiple strikes that might achieve desired goals. Frequency is an important factor when choosing to embark on a strike. A longer pause between hunger strikes (as was the case with the 2004 and 2012 strikes) along with different strategic planning caused public support for the prisoners to swell. When the frequency of hunger strikes is high, it can cause fatigue among the wider public (which, in turn, dissipates support) and among prisoners and their allies. By refraining from overusing the tactic, prison activists can better mobilize participants inside prisons and allies outside prisons and thus improve the efficacy of the strike.

Hold Awareness Sessions

Matters of success and efficacy should also be a subject of deliberation within the incarcerated community before undertaking a hunger strike. Awareness-raising sessions are needed to answer difficult questions about whether hunger strikes are needed and whether they can bring about the desired outcomes in the particular circumstances of the prisoners. They also allow prisoners to learn how to best maintain their health and what to expect from their bodies while undergoing the strike. Such sessions effectively bring forth the voices of hunger strikers and their families. They create an occasion to identify new tactical choices or opportunities and new ways of embarking on hunger strikes.

Minimize the Risks

Finally, it is important for a prison hunger striker to be able to minimize, to the greater extent possible, the danger they pose to themselves and their fellow prisoners, without compromising the effectiveness of their strike. Must a prison hunger striker approach death to gain leverage over the terms of their incarceration? Our research suggests that effective hunger strikes can be waged even when death is neither a likely nor a necessary outcome. The more international scrutiny the hunger action gains, and the more transnational solidarity that hunger strikers acquire, the greater the chance hunger strikers have of changing the dynamics of their imprisonment, and thereby altering the conditions of incarceration for themselves and others.

Recommendations for Future Study

Prison life tends to remain unknown to the outside world. Knowledge concerning what happens inside is shared with few practitioners, often only lawyers and state officials, who rarely publish their research or record their experience for the public. Also, many observers fail to recognize the extent to which the fate of political prisoners is affected by shifts in geopolitical alignments. With these gaps in mind, we recommend that future studies focus on the dynamics of prison hunger strikes in more granular detail. An interdisciplinary approach is also needed. Anthropology, sociology, history, and political science should all be put to the service of illuminating the hunger striker's struggle and the conditions for their success. At present, however, Cold War and post–Cold War alignments dominate and obscure the discussion, preventing and obstructing the transnational solidarities that are so crucial to hunger strikes' success.

Although this study builds on and revises classical paradigms around nonviolent resistance in the context of hunger strikes, it largely refrains from tracking the entanglement of prisoners in international geopolitics. Yet, hunger strikers in Iranian prisons, for example, are regularly instrumentalized by geopolitical agendas premised on US–Iranian hostility. Likewise, the Israeli authorities label Palestinian prisoners as "security prisoners," and this narrative is often accepted and internalized by local and international media, including by sources that conceive of themselves as neutral or even sympathetic to the Palestinian cause. Moving beyond classifications and labels that rely on discourses of securitization is necessary to see incarceration sites for what they are: violent, dehumanizing, and inhumane spaces. Future research should investigate the effects of the geopolitical context on the prison hunger strike experience: what opportunities it may create, and what challenges it brings.

Our analysis of prison hunger strikes is also an invitation for all our readers to reimagine the process of decolonization. The strategies developed by Palestinian hunger strikers to challenge the conditions of their occupation should serve as an inspiration to everyone who wants to fight global injustice, with their ideas as well as with their bodies.

Appendix: List of Interviews

Since some interviewees participated in more than one interview, the date mentioned refers to the last interview conducted. Also, some interviewees were traveling while interviewed, hence they referred to the country of the place where they were located during the interview, not to the country of their permanent residence. All interviews were conducted by Malaka Shwaikh, unless otherwise noted. "Ex" in ex-prisoners/hunger strikers means they are no longer prisoners/hunger strikers at the time of the interviews, and the absence of "ex" means they are prisoners/hunger strikers at that time.

1. Fahed Abu al-Haj, ex-Palestinian hunger striker, voice call, 2018.

2. Monqiz Abu Atwan, ex-Palestinian hunger striker, voice call, 2018.

3. Anas Abu Khudair, ex-prisoner and hunger striker, face-to-face interview, Amman, Jordan, 2016.

4. Khader Adnan, ex-Palestinian prisoner and hunger striker, voice interview, WhatsApp, 2016.

5. Ahmed al-Faleet, ex-Palestinian hunger striker, Facebook messenger, 2018.

6. Fouad al-Qafash, ex-Palestinian prisoner and hunger striker, WhatsApp and Facebook, 2018.

7. Hussam Badran, ex-Palestinian hunger striker, face-to-face interview in Doha, 2018.

8. Qassam Barghouti, son of Fatah leader in Israeli prisons Marwan Barghouti, Facebook messenger, 2018.

9. Moazzam Begg, ex-British prisoner in Guantánamo prison and ex-hunger striker, face-to-face interview in Belfast, 2016.

10. Etaf Elian, ex-prisoner and first individual documented female hunger striker in Israeli prisons since 1967, Facebook, 2018.

11. Suaad Genem, ex-Palestinian prisoner and hunger striker, face-to-face interview in Exeter, 2018.

12. Ala' Hamad, wife of Abdullah Hamad, Palestinian-Jordanian prisoner and ex-hunger striker in Israeli prisons, face-to-face interview in Jordan, 2016.

13. Ra'fat Hamdouna, ex-Palestinian hunger striker, via WhatsApp, 2018.

14. Shireen Issawi, Palestinian hunger striker and sister of Samer Issawi, WhatsApp, 2018.

15. Mazin Malasa, Palestinian-Jordanian hunger striker, face-to-face interview in Amman, 2016.

16. Shireen Nafie, prisoners' activist, face-to-face interview, in Amman, 2016.

17. Julie Norman, Teaching Fellow in Politics and International Relations based in the UK, face-to-face interview in Belfast (Queen's University), 2018.

18. Mona Qa'dan, ex-Palestinian hunger striker, online messages, 2020.

19. Essam Qadmani, ex-Palestinian hunger striker, face-to-face interview in Doha, 2018.

20. Muntaha Qassem, wife of Abdullah Hamad, Palestinian-Jordanian prisoner and ex-hunger striker in Israeli prisons, face-to-face interview, Jordan, 2016.

21. Um Ra'afat, mother of Samer Issawi, 2012 (see also Shwaikh 2013).

22. Nilly Safadi, ex-Palestinian prisoner and wife of ex-hunger striker Obada Bilal, face-to-face interview in Amman, 2016.

23. Amani Sarahna, media coordinator in the PPSMO, WhatsApp, 2016–2018.

24. Mahmoud Sarsak, ex-Palestinian hunger striker, face-to-face interviews in London, 2016–2018.

25. Hana Shalabi, ex-Palestinian hunger striker, Facebook, 2018.

26. Pat Sheehan, former IRA prisoner and hunger striker, face-to-face interview in Belfast, 2016.

Works Cited

1. Legal Documents

Fourth Geneva Convention. "Article 76: Treatment of Detainees." In *Convention (IV) relative to the Protection of Civilian Persons in Time of War.* Geneva, 12 August 1949. Commentary of 1957. **https://ihl-databases.icrc.org/en/ihl-treaties /gciv-1949/article-76/commentary/1958**.

Good Friday Agreement. *The Belfast Agreement: An Agreement Reached at the Multi-Party Talks on Northern Ireland.* April 1998. **https://assets.publishing.service.gov.uk /government/uploads/system/uploads /attachment_data/file/136652/agreement.pdf**.

High Court of Justice of England and Wales. *Ministry of Defence and Support for Armed Forces of the Islamic Republic of Iran v. International Military Services Limited.* 2019.

International Covenant on Civil and Political Rights [ICCPR]. Article 9(1). **https://www.ohchr.org/en/special -procedures/sr-religion-or-belief/international -standards**.

Iranian Penal Code (Qanun-i Jarm siyasi). *Political Crimes Law.* **https://rc.majlis.ir/fa/law/show/968421** (4.3.1395).

Peace Agreements & Related. *Israeli-Palestinian Interim Agreement (Oslo II). Annex VII: Release of Palestinian Prisoners and Detainees.* September 28, 1995. **https://www.refworld.org/docid/3de5ed521 .html**.

United States Supreme Court. *Boumediene v Bush (President of the United States), Decision, Docket No 06-1195, 553 US 723 (2008), 128 S. Ct. 2229 (2008), ILDC 1039 (US 2008).* June 12, 2008.

2. Film and Video Sources

Al-Atrash, Mirna. "On Awni al-Sheikh." *Maan Network.* November 24, 2015. **https://www.youtube.com/watch?v =uNbWYvN09e0**.

Al Jazeera. "On Dima al-Wawi." *Al Jazeera.* May 4, 2016. **https://www.youtube.com/watch?v= rcbxtgx6tWE**.

Al-Mayadeen. "Honoring Djamila Bouhaired." 1993. **https://www.youtube.com/watch?v= YThQ8W95qU0**.

Al-Qafash, Fouad, in Mashharawi 2014.

Al-Sharawna, Ayman, in Mashharawi 2014.

Habash, Shireen Moussa. "[Al-Naqab Prison, Known as Ansar III, is One of the Largest Prisons of the Occupation]." *Palestine 27k.* YouTube video. March 2, 2019. **https://www.youtube.com/watch?v=_ n7NNuw8i6o**.

Jewish Voice for Peace [JVP]. "Angela Davis on Democracy Now!" Twitter video. June 15, 2020. **https://twitter.com/jvplive/status /1272560387418927104**.

Maan Network. "The Youngest Prisoner in the World: Dima al-Wawi." 2016. **https://www.youtube.com/watch?v= alzwki7fpJc**.

Mashharawi, Ashraf. "Video: Hunger Strike – To What Length Do Palestinian Prisoners in Israel Go on Hunger Strike." *Al Jazeera*. August 13, 2014. **https://www.youtube.com/watch?v= u49jwfcLwuE**.

McFarlane, Brendan, in Mashharawi 2014.

Nassar, Mithal, in Mashharawi 2014.

Shalabi, Hanah, in Mashharawi 2014.

Sheehan, Pat, in Mashharawi 2014.

Takruri, Dina. "Ahed Tamimi: Palestine's Freedom Fighter, Pt. 2." *AJ+*. October 9, 2018. **https://m.youtube.com/watch?v=IJqH7 _xYKi4**.

University of California Television [UCTV]. "Free Angela and All Political Prisoners." *UCTV*. January 7, 2014. **https://www.youtube.com/watch?v=N1wr -BXtIW0**.

Ziv, Ilan, director. *People Power.* New York: Icarus/Tamouz Media, 1989.

3. Bibliography

Abdalla, Amr, and Yasmine Arafa. "Egypt: Nonviolent Resistance in the Rise of a Nation-State, 1805–1922." In *Recovering Nonviolent History: Civil Resistance in Liberation Struggles*, edited by Maciej Bartkowski, 125–141. Boulder: Lynne Rienner Publishers, 2013.

Abdo, Nahla. *Captive Revolution: Palestinian Women's Anti-Colonial Struggle Within the Israeli Prison System*. London: Pluto Press, 2014.

Abu Arafeh, Khaled. *[Palestinian Resistance Against Israeli Occupation in Jerusalem, 1987–2015]*. Beirut: Al-Zaytouna Centre for Studies and Consultations, 2017.

Abu Atwan, Monqiz. *Institutionalization of the Imprisonment Life for Palestinian Prisoners in Israeli Jails Between 1967–2005*. MA thesis. Ramallah: Birzeit University, 2007.

Abu Ghoush, Ahmed, Attia Adnan, and Qadri Abu Baker. *Palestinian Detainees*. Ramallah: Al-Awda for Studies and Publishing, 2004.

Abu Laban, Reem. "How Do Women Deal with Their Monthly Periods While in Israeli Interrogation Rooms." *Al-Hadath*. November 25, 2016. **https://tinyurl.com/4b2fka5z**.

Abusalama, Shahd. "How My Father Survived a Hunger Strike in Israel." *Al Jazeera*. May 30, 2017. **https://www.aljazeera.com/indepth /features/2017/05/father-survived-hunger -strike-israel-170523063347512.html**.

Abusalama, Shahd. "'The First Day is the Hardest': Ex-prisoner Loai Odeh's Hunger Strike Diary." *Electronic Intifada*. April 25, 2012. **https://electronicintifada.net/blogs/shahd -abusalama/first-day-hardest-ex-prisoner -loai-odehs-hunger-strike-diary**.

Abu Samra, Qais. "[The Palestinian Prisoner: Facts and Figures (Framework)]." *Anadolu Agency*. April 16, 2020. **https://www.aa.com.tr/ar/الأسير-التقارير/ الفلسطينيحقائق-وأرقام-إطار/1806717**.

95

Abu Sneineh, Mustafa. "Beds, Kettles and Books: How Hunger Strikes Changed the Cells of Palestinian Prisoners." *Middle East Eye.* May 1, 2019. **https://www.middleeasteye.net/news/beds-kettles-and-books-how-hunger-strikes-changed-cells-palestinian-prisoners.**

Adalah. "Palestinian Citizens of Israel: A Primer." *Adalah.* July 7, 2019. **https://www.adalah.org/en/content/view/9271.**

Adams, Robert. *Prison Riots in Britain and the USA,* 2nd ed. London: Palgrave, 1994.

Addameer Report. *Annual Violations Report, 2019.* Ramallah: Addameer, 2020. **http://www.addameer.org/sites/default/files/publications/v2020_online.pdf.**

Addameer. "Ashkelon (Askalan) Central Prison & Prison Building." No date (a). **https://www.addameer.org/content/shikma-prison.**

Addameer. "Imprisonment of Children." December 2017a. **http://www.addameer.org/the_prisoners/children.**

Addameer. "Prisons and Detention Centers." No date (b). **http://www.addameer.org/prisons-and-detention-centers.**

Addameer. "Ramleh Prison & Clinic." No date (c). **http://www.addameer.org/prisons/ramleh-prison-clinic.**

Addameer. "Restrictions on Family Visits." July 2017b. **http://www.addameer.org/key_issues/family_visit.**

Addameer. *Solitary Confinement and Isolation.* No date (d). **http://www.addameer.org/sites/default/files/publications/fact_sheet_on_solitary_confinement_and_isolation_002.pdf.**

Addameer. "Statistics." Accessed September 2022. **http://www.addameer.org/statistics.**

Addameer. *Violations Against Palestinian Prisoners in Israeli Prisons and Detention Centers.* Annual Report. Ramallah: Addameer, 2013. **https://www.addameer.org/sites/default/files/publications/al_dameer_annual_report_english.pdf.**

Adiv, Sylvia. "Political Prisoners in the Infernal Jails." In *Haolam Hlazeb,* May 14, 1975. Quoted in *Treatment of Palestinians in Israeli-Occupied West Bank and Gaza: Report of the National Lawyers Guild 1977 Middle East Delegation.* New York: National Lawyers Guild, 1978.

Ajour, Ashjan. *Reclaiming Humanity in Palestinian Hunger Strikes: Revolutionary Subjectivity and Decolonizing the Body.* New York: Springer, 2021.

Al-Aissa, Osama. "[On Awni al-Sheikh]." Blogspot blogpost. January 29, 2015. **http://alrawwya.blogspot.com/2015/01/blog-post_29.html.**

Al-Assa, Fadi. "[Palestinian Prisoners' Hunger Strikes: Freedom or Martyrdom]." *Al Jazeera.* April 7, 2019. **http://aljazeera.net/news/politics/2019/4/7/الأسرى-إضراب-فلسطين-عن-الطعام-حرية/**

Alexander, Michelle. *The New Jim Crow: Mass Incarceration in the Age of Colorblindness.* New York: New Press, 2018.

Al-Qaimari, Atta. *The Prison is Not for Us.* Nafha Prison, 1981.

Al-Laithi, Muhammad. "Mona Qadan: The Strike Will Bear Fruit, and the Occupation Uses 'Force Feeding' That Leads to Death." *El Watan News.* May 2, 2017. **https://www.elwatannews.com/news/details/2058301.**

Allen, Lori. "Getting by the Occupation: How Violence Became Normal During the Second Palestinian Intifada." *Cultural Anthropology* 23, no. 3 (2008): 453–487.

Allen, Lori. *The Rise and Fall of Human Rights: Cynicism and Politics in Occupied Palestine*. Stanford: Stanford University Press, 2013.

Al-Mayadeen. "[Prisoner Khader Adnan is Free After 25 Days of Hunger Strike]." *Al-Mayadeen Net*. June 28, 2021. **https://www.almayadeen.net/news/politics /1491155/الأسير-خضر-عدنان-حرا-بعد-يوما-من- الإضراب-عن-الطعام**

Al-Nabulsi, Muna. "[Hunger Strikes by Palestinian Prisoners: Opportunities of Success and Potentials of Failure]." *Al-Akhbar*. April 27, 2017. **https://al-akhbar.com/Opinion/229788**.

Al-Rimmawi, Hussein, and Esmat A. Zaidan. "Effect of Demographic Factor on Palestinian– Israeli Conflict." *International Journal of Humanities and Social Science* 3, no. 6 (2013): 214–224.

Alsaafin, Linah. "I Was Force-Fed by Israel in the '70s: This is My Story." *Middle East Eye*. August 15, 2015. **http://www.middleeasteye.net/news/former -palestinian-prisoner-recounts-experience -force-feeding-45-years-ago-2078639559**.

Amini, Mehdi. "Free Nasrin Sotoudeh NOW!" Online petition. *Change.org*. 2019. **https://www.change.org/p/free-nasrin -sotoudeh-now**.

Amnesty International. "Trade Unionist Punished for Hunger Strike: Shahrokh Zamani." *Amnesty International*. April 16, 2014. **https://www.amnesty.org/en/documents /MDE13/019/2014/en/**.

Amnesty International UK. "Iranian Filmmaker and Musicians Jailed After Three-Minute Trial." *Amnesty International UK*. May 18, 2020. **https://www.amnesty.org.uk/iranian -filmmaker-and-musicians-jailed-after-three -minute-trial**.

Andriolo, Karin. "The Twice-Killed: Imagining Protest Suicide." *American Anthropologist* 108, no. 1 (2006): 100–113. **https://anthrosource.onlinelibrary.wiley.com /doi/abs/10.1525/aa.2006.108.1.100**.

Anqawi, Helmi. *The First Stages of Imprisonment*. Al-Ghad Library, 1995.

Anthony, Charles B. "Meet Mohamed Soltan: The 500-day Hunger Striker Who Survived a Massacre." *Middle East Eye*. December 2, 2015. **https://www.middleeasteye.net/news/meet -mohamed-soltan-500-day-hunger-striker -who-survived-massacre**.

Antonius, Soraya. "Prisoners for Palestine: A List of Women Political Prisoners." *Journal of Palestine Studies* 9, no. 3 (1980): 29–80.

Arendt, Hannah. *Crises of the Republic: Lying in Politics; Civil Disobedience; On Violence; Thoughts on Politics and Revolution*. New York: Harcourt Brace, 1972.

Ashe, Thomas. *The Death of Thomas Ashe: Full Report of the Inquest*. Dublin: J. M. Butler, 1917.

Assiter, Alison. "Hunger Strikes, Iran and Universal Human Rights." *E-International Relations*. 18 July 2019. **https://www.e-ir.info/2019/07/18/hunger -strikes-iran-and-universal-human-rights/**.

Atack, Iain. *Nonviolence in Political Theory*. Edinburgh: Edinburgh University Press, 2012.

Ayyash, M. Muhannad. "What is Israel's Word Worth?" *Al Jazeera*. December 7, 2021. **https://www.aljazeera.com/opinions/2021 /12/7/what-is-israels-word-worth**.

Azoulay, Ariella. *Potential History: Unlearning Imperialism*. London: Verso, 2019.

Bab el-Wad. "[A Brief History of Prison Break in Palestine]." *Bab el-Wad*. April 27, 2017. **https://babelwad.com/ar/فلسطين/houroub -men-elsejen-part-2-3/**.

Baker, Abeer, and Anat Matar. *Threat: Palestinian Political Prisoners in Israel*. London: Pluto Press, 2011.

Bakri, Qasim. "Captive al-Issawi is on Hunger Strike in Solidarity with Captive Allan." *Arab 48*. August 18, 2015. **https://www.arab48.com/فلسطينيات /أخبار/2015/08/18/الأسيرة-العيساوي-تضرب-عن- الطعام-تضامنا-مع-الأسير-علان.**

Barberis, Peter, John McHugh, and Mike Tyldesley. *Encyclopedia of British and Irish Political Organisations: Parties, Groups, and Movements of the Twentieth Century*. London: Bloomsbury, 2000.

Barghouti, Marwan. "Why We Are on Hunger Strike in Israel's Prisons." *New York Times*. April 16, 2017. **https://www.nytimes.com/2017/04/16 /opinion/palestinian-hunger-strike-prisoners -call-for-justice.html.**

Barghouti, Omar. *Boycott, Divestment, Sanctions: The Global Struggle for Palestinian Rights*. Chicago: Haymarket Books, 2011.

Bargu, Banu. "Forging Life into a Weapon." *Social Text Online*. May 21, 2011. **https://socialtextjournal.org/periscope _article/the_weaponization_of_life_-_banu _bargu/.**

Bargu, Banu. *Starve and Immolate: The Politics of Human Weapons*. New York: Columbia University Press, 2014.

Bargu, Banu. "The Silent Exception: Hunger Striking and Lip-Sewing." *Law, Culture and the Humanities* 18, no. 2 (2017). **http://journals.sagepub.com/doi /abs/10.1177/1743872117709684.**

Baumann, Marcel. "Transforming Conflict Toward and Away from Violence: Bloody Sunday and the Hunger Strikes in Northern Ireland." *Dynamics of Asymmetric Conflict: Pathways Toward Terrorism and Genocide* 2, no. 3 (2009): 172–180.

Baynes, Megan. "Nazanin Zaghari-Ratcliffe Ends Hunger Strike in Prison After 15 Days, Prompting Husband to End Protest." *The Telegraph*. June 29, 2019.

BBC. "Ahed Tamimi: Palestinian Slap Video Teen Gets Eight Months in Plea Deal." March 21, 2018. **https://www.bbc.co.uk/news/world-middle -east-43487885.**

Beaumont, Peter. "Palestinians Renew Calls to Free 'Leader-in-Waiting' Marwan Barghouti." *The Guardian*. March 26, 2014. **https://www.theguardian.com/world/2014 /mar/26/palestinians-renew-calls-free -marwan-barghouti.**

Begg, Moazzam, and Victoria Brittain. *Enemy Combatant: My Imprisonment at Guantanamo, Bagram, and Kandahar*. New York: New Press, 2007.

Benjamin, Walter. "Theses on the Philosophy of History." In *Illuminations*, 253–264, translated by Harry Zohn. New York: Schocken, 1968.

Beresford, David. *Ten Men Dead: The Story of the 1981 Irish Hunger Strike*. New York: Harper Collins, 1987.

Berger, Miriam. "Israeli Force-Feeding Law Pits Doctors Against State." *Associated Press*. August 14, 2015. **https://bit.ly/2pRhtxA.**

Biddle, Sam. "Facebook Report Concludes Company Censorship Violated Palestinian Human Rights." *The Intercept.* September 21, 2022. **https://theintercept.com/2022/09/21 /facebook-censorship-palestine-israel -algorithm/**.

Borders, William. "Belfast Prisoners End Hunger Strike That Left 10 Dead." *New York Times.* October 4, 1981. **https://www.nytimes.com/1981/10/04/world /belfast-prisoners-end-hunger-strike-that-left -10-dead.html**.

Borman, William. *Gandhi and Non-Violence.* Albany: SUNY Press, 1986.

Boumediene, Lakhdar. "I Was Force-Fed at Guantanamo. What Guards Are Doing Now Is Worse." *New Republic.* 2017. **https://newrepublic.com/article/145549 /force-fed-guantanamo-guards-now-worse**.

Boumediene, Lakhdar, and Mustafa Ait Idir. *Witnesses of the Unseen: Seven Years in Guantanamo.* Stanford: Stanford University Press, 2018.

Bowcott, Owen. "Hope Dies in Turkish Prison Hunger Strike." *The Guardian.* January 18, 2002. **https://www.theguardian.com/world/2002 /jan/19/owenbowcott**.

Breiner, Josh. "Israel Prison Service Says More Palestinians Injured in Riot Than First Reported." *Haaretz.* January 28, 2019b. **https://www.haaretz.com/israel-news /.premium-israel-prison-service-revises -number-of-palestinians-injured-in -riot-1.6877526**.

Breiner, Josh. "Six Palestinian Inmates, Three Guards Wounded in Riots at Three Israeli Prisons." *Haaretz.* January 21, 2019a. **https://www.haaretz.com/israel-news /.premium-six-palestinian-inmates-three -guards-wounded-in-riots-at-three-israeli -prisons-1.6866077**.

B'Tselem. "[Administrative Detainee Hana Shalabi is Entering the 40th Day of Her Hunger Strike]." *B'Tselem.* March 26, 2012. **https://www.btselem.org/arabic /administrative_detention/hana_shalabi**.

B'Tselem. "Administrative Detention." *B'Tselem.* 2017. **https://www.btselem.org/administrative _detention**.

Center for Human Rights in Iran [CHRI]. "Imprisoned Labor Activist Dies of Stroke After Being Denied Medical Care." *CHRI.* September 15, 2015. **https://www.iranhumanrights.org/2015/09 /shahrokh-zamani-death/**.

Center for Human Rights in Iran. "Mass Hunger Strike Launched in Evin Prison Against Unlawful Treatment of Political Prisoners." *CHRI.* July 18, 2019. **https://www.iranhumanrights.org/2019/07 /mass-hunger-strike-launched-in-evin-prison -against-unlawful-treatment-of-political -prisoners/**.

Center for Human Rights in Iran. "Nasrin Sotoudeh and Baha'i Political Prisoner Refuse Phone Calls in Solidarity with Nazanin Zaghari-Ratcliffe." *CHRI.* January 11, 2019. **https://iranhumanrights.org/2019/01/nasrin -sotoudeh-and-bahai-political-prisoner -refuse-phone-calls-in-solidarity-with -nazanin-zaghari-ratcliffe/**.

Center for Human Rights in Iran. "Parliament Faction Links Lacking Accountability to Deaths of Political Prisoners in State Custody." *CHRI.* July 8, 2019. **https://iranhumanrights.org/2019/07/iran -parliament-faction-links-lacking-accountability -to-deaths-of-political-prisoners-in-state -custody/**.

Center for Human Rights in Iran. "Political Prisoner Ali Shariati Tricked into Ending Hunger Strike with False Promise by Judiciary." *CHRI.* July 12, 2017. https://www.iranhumanrights.org/2017/07/political-prisoner-ali-shariati-tricked-into-ending-hunger-strike-with-false-promise-by-judiciary/.

Chabot, Sean, and Majid Sharifi. "The Violence of Nonviolence: Problematizing Nonviolent Resistance in Iran and Egypt." *Societies Without Borders* 8, no. 2 (2013): 205–232.

Chenoweth, Erica, and Maria J. Stephan. *Why Civil Resistance Works: The Strategic Logic of Nonviolent Conflict.* New York: Columbia University Press, 2011.

Claiborne, William. "2d Prisoner Dies After Israelis Force-Fed Arabs." *Washington Post.* July 25, 1980. https://wapo.st/2K5lbPx.

Cochrane, Feargal. *Unionist Politics and the Politics of Unionism Since the Anglo-Irish Agreement.* Cork: Cork University Press, 1997.

Connelly, Mark. *The IRA on Film and Television: A History.* Jefferson: McFarland and Company, 2014.

Coogan, Tim Pat. *The IRA: A History.* Boulder: Roberts Rinehart Publishers, 1993.

Corkery, Claire. "British Council Worker Aras Amiri 'Discovered Her Jail Sentence on Iranian TV.'" *The National.* July 17, 2019. https://www.thenationalnews.com/world/mena/british-council-worker-aras-amiri-discovered-her-jail-sentence-on-iranian-tv-1.887471.

Crawford, Elizabeth. *The Women's Suffrage Movement: A Reference Guide, 1866–1928.* London: Routledge, 2003.

Cummins, Eric. *The Rise and Fall of California's Radical Prison Movement.* Stanford: Stanford University Press, 1994.

Dakka, Waleed. "صهر الوعي [Molding of Consciousness]." *Sahar al-Waee.* 2009. http://www.safsaf.org/12-2009/asra/walid-dakkah.htm.

Dao, James. "A Nation Challenged: Guantánamo; Navy Doctors Force-Feeding 2 Prisoners." *New York Times.* April 2, 2002.

Davis, Angela Y. *Are Prisons Obsolete?* New York: Seven Stories, 2003.

Denniston, Lyle. "US Defines Its Claim to Detention Power." *SCOTUSblog.* March 13, 2009. https://www.scotusblog.com/2009/03/us-defines-its-claim-to-detention-power/#more-8978.

Dudouet, Véronique, ed. *Civil Resistance and Conflict Transformation: Transitions from Armed to Nonviolent Struggle,* London: Routledge, 2015.

Ellmann, Maud. *The Hunger Artists: Starving, Writing, and Imprisonment.* Cambridge: Harvard University Press, 1993.

Fanon, Mahmoud. *The Philosophy of Confrontation Behind Bars.* Dar Ar-raya, 1982.

Farraj, Basil. "How Palestinian Hunger Strikes Counter Israel's Monopoly on Violence." *Al-Shabaka.* May 12, 2016. https://al-shabaka.org/commentaries/palestinian-hunger-strikes-counter-israels-monopoly-violence/.

Farwana, Abd al-Naser. "[Prisoners Between Division and Reconciliation]." *Maan News.* October 13, 2017. https://www.maannews.net/Content.aspx?id=925588.

Fiala, Andrew. *The Routledge Handbook of Pacifism and Nonviolence.* Abingdon: Routledge, 2018.

Fierke, K. M. *Political Self-Sacrifice: Agency, Body and Emotion in International Relations.* Cambridge: Cambridge University Press, 2012.

Foucault, Michel. "Useless to Revolt?" In *Ethics: Subjectivity and Truth (The Essential Works of Foucault, 1954–1984, vol. 1)*, edited by Paul Rainbow, 449–453. New York: The New Press, 1979.

Fox, Gemma. "Israel Refuses to Release Palestinian 'on Verge of Death" After Almost 80 Day Hunger Strike." *The Independent.* October 13, 2020. **https://www.independent.co.uk/news/world /middle-east/maher-al-akhras-hunger-strike -palestine-israel-west-bank-islamic-jihad -ahlam-haddad-b1013558.html**.

Francis, Sahar. "Gendered Violence in Israeli Detention." *Journal of Palestine Studies* 46, no. 4 (2017): 46–61.

Gamson, William. "Measuring Movement Outcomes." *Mobilizing Ideas* blogpost. January 1, 2014. **https://mobilizingideas.wordpress .com/2014/01/01/measuring-movement -outcomes/**.

Gamson, William A. *The Strategy of Social Protest,* 2nd ed. Belmont: Wadsworth, 1990.

Gillan, Audrey. "Hunger Strikers Pledge to Die in Guantánamo." *The Guardian.* September 8, 2005. **https://www.theguardian.com/world/2005 /sep/09/uk.guantanamo**.

Gilmore, Ruth Wilson. *Change Everything: Racial Capitalism and the Case for Abolition.* Chicago: Haymarket Books, 2021.

Gould, Rebecca. *Writers and Rebels: The Literature of Insurgency in the Caucasus.* New Haven and London: Yale University Press, 2016.

Gramsci, Antonio. *Selections from the Prison Notebooks.* Edited and translated by Quentin Hoare and Geoffrey Nowell Smith. London: International Publishers, 1971.

Green, Penny. "Turkish Jails, Hunger Strikes and the European Drive for Prison Reform." *Punishment & Society* 4, no. 1 (2002): 97–101.

Habermas, Jürgen. "Civil Disobedience: Litmus Test for the Democratic Constitutional State." *Berkeley Journal of Sociology* 30 (1985): 95–116.

Hamdan, Hashim. "[Prisoners Shireen and Medhat Al-Issawi Suspend Their Hunger Strike]." *Arab 48.* June 20, 2015. **https://www.arab48.com/-الحركة/فلسطينيات الأسيرة/2015/06/20/الأسيران-شيرين-ومدحت- العيساوي-يعلقان-إضرابهما-عن-الطعام.**

Hass, Amira. *Drinking the Sea at Gaza: Days and Nights in a Land Under Siege.* New York: Henry Holt and Company, 2014.

Hass, Amira. "Otherwise Occupied: For Israel, It Seems Goliath was the Victim." *Haaretz.* July 27, 2015. **https://www.haaretz.com/.premium-goliath -the-victim-1.5379470**.

Hassan, Budour Youssef. "Shackled to a Bed, Starving for Freedom." *The Electronic Intifada.* May 13, 2016. **https://electronicintifada.net/content /shackled-bed-starving-freedom/16681**.

Hawari, Yara. "The Systematic Torture of Palestinians in Israeli Detention." *Al-Shabaka.* November 28, 2019. **https://al-shabaka.org/briefs/the-systematic -torture-of-palestinians-in-israeli-detention/**.

Holmes, Oliver, and Sufian Taha. "Ahed Tamimi: 'I Am a Freedom Fighter. I Will Not Be the Victim.'" *The Guardian.* July 30, 2018. **https://www.theguardian.com/world/2018 /jul/30/ahed-tamimi-i-am-a-freedom-fighter -i-will-not-be-the-victim-palestinian-israel**.

Holmes, Robert L. *Pacifism: A Philosophy of Nonviolence.* London: Bloomsbury, 2016.

Horowitz, Adam, Lizzy Ratner, and Philip Weiss. *The Goldstone Report: The Legacy of the Landmark Investigation of the Gaza Conflict.* New York: Nation Books, 2011.

Hosseinioun, Mishana. *The Human Rights Turn and the Paradox of Progress in the Middle East.* New York: Springer, 2017.

Hughes, William John. "The Longevity of Religious Terrorist Organisations." Bard College. *Senior Projects Spring 2017,* no. 229 (2017). **https://digitalcommons.bard.edu/cgi /viewcontent .cgi?article=1219&context =senproj_s2017.**

Human Rights Activists News Agency. "وحید صیادی نصیری، زندانی سیاسی در پی اعتصاب اذا [Vahid Sayadi Nasiri, در زندان قم جان باخت a Political Prisoner, Died in Qom Prison Following a Hunger Strike]." 2019. **https://www.hra-news.org/2018 /hranews/a-18246/(١٢/٩٠/٧٩٣١).**

Human Rights Watch [HRW]. "Palestine: Crackdown on Journalists, Activists." August 29, 2016. **https://www.hrw.org/news/2016/08/30 /palestine-crackdown-journalists-activists.**

Hunter, Molly, and Nasser Atta. "Palestinian Teen Activist Could Face Years in Prison After Slapping an Israeli Soldier." *ABC News.* December 20, 2017. **https://abcnews.go.com/International /palestinian-teen-activist-face-years-prison -slapping-israeli/story?id=51913049.**

Hurewitz, J. C. *The Struggle for Palestine.* New York: Schocken Books, 1976.

Hussain, Nasser. "Beyond Norm and Exception: Guantánamo." *Critical Inquiry* 33, no. 4 (2007): 734–753.

Ibrahim, Yasmin, and Anita Howarth. "Hunger Strike and the Force-Feeding Chair: Guantanamo Bay and Corporeal Surrender." *Environment and Planning D: Society and Space* 37, no. 2 (2019): 294–312.

International Council Supporting Fair Trial and Human Rights [ICSFT]. "[Full Text of the Message of the Dean of Prisoners, Karim Younis: Either Victory or Martyrdom!" 2017. **http://www.icsft.net/8022/.**

International Middle East Media Center [IMEMC]. "Samer al-Issawi Re-arrested." *IMEMC News.* June 24, 2014. **https://imemc.org/article/68203/.**

Israeli Chanel 10 [IC10]. "Interview with the Legal Advisor to the Israeli Ministry of Public Security, Yoel Adar." March 2, 2014. Cited in Addameer, "Factsheet: Force-Feeding Under International Law and Medical Standards," November 16, 2015.

Issawi, Samer. "Samer Issawi's 'Hunger Speech' to Israelis." *Mondoweiss.* April 9, 2013a. **https://mondoweiss.net/2013/04/issawis -speech-israelis/.**

Issawi, Samer. "We Are Fighting for All Palestinians." *the Guardian,* 2013b. **https://www.theguardian.com /commentisfree/2013/mar/03/hunger -strikers-fighting-for-palestinians-israel.**

Jaradat, Ali. "*Shahid li-l-haraka al-asira* [Abdul Qader Abu Al-Fahem: The First Martyr of the Prisoners Movement]." *Majallat al-Dirasat al-Filastiniyya* 22, no. 85 (2011): 145–48. **https://www.palestine-studies.org/en /node/37849.**

Johns, Fleur. "Guantánamo Bay and the Annihilation of the Exception." *European Journal of International Law* 16, no. 4 (2005): 613–635.

Kallen, Stuart. *We Are Not Beasts of Burden: Cesar Chavez and the Delano Grape Strike, California, 1965–1970.* Minneapolis: Twenty-First Century Books, 2010.

Kamali Dehghan, Saeed. "Letter from Ex-PM About Jailed British-Iranian Woman 'Proves Government' Links.'" *The Guardian.* October 17, 2017. **https://www.theguardian.com/world/2017 /oct/17/letter-from-ex-pm-about-jailed-british -iranian-woman-proves-government-links**.

Kawas, Marion. "Ansar: A Testament to the Ugly Brutality of the Israeli Jailer." *Palestine Chronicle.* April 14, 2020. **https://www.palestinechronicle.com/ansar-a -testament-to-the-ugly-brutality-of-the-israeli -jailer/**.

Keddie, Nikki. *Iran: Religion, Politics, and Society: Collected Essays.* London: Routledge, 2013.

Khamis, Tariq. "Awni Sheikh: The Old Man Who Fought Alone." *Quds News Network.* June 15, 2013. **https://www.qudsn.co/article/18098.**

Khazan, Olga. "Why the Guantanamo Bay Hunger Strikes Probably Won't Work." *The Atlantic.* April 2, 2013. **https://www.theatlantic.com/international /archive/2013/04/why-the-guantanamo-bay -hunger-strikes-probably-wont-work/274561/**.

Khosrokhavar, Farhad. *New Arab Revolutions That Shook the World.* Abingdon: Routledge, 2016.

Khoury, Jack. "Palestinian Official: Deal to End Prisoners' Hunger Strike Not a Victory." *Haaretz.* June 25, 2014. **https://www.haaretz.com/.premium-deal-to -end-hunger-strike-not-a-victory-1.5253277.**

King, Martin Luther, Jr. "A Time to Break Silence." Speech at Riverside Church Meeting, New York, April 4, 1967. In *The Eyes on the Prize Civil Rights Reader: Documents Speeches, and Firsthand Accounts from the Black Freedom Struggle*, edited by Clayborne Caron, David J. Garrow, Gerald Gill, Vincent Harding, and Darlene Clark Hine, 387–393. New York: Penguin Books, 1987.

King, Martin Luther, Jr. "Letter from Birmingham Jail." In *Civil Disobedience in Focus*, edited by Hugo Adam Bedau, 68–84. London: Routledge, 1991.

King, Mary Elizabeth. *A Quiet Revolution: The First Palestinian Intifada and Nonviolent Resistance.* New York: Nation Books, 2007.

Knight, Lionel. *Britain in India, 1858–1947.* London: Anthem Press, 2012.

Kuttab, Daoud. "Kidnapping Prompts Palestinian Prisoners to End Hunger Strike." *Al-Monitor.* June 26, 2014. **http://www.almonitor.com/pulse /originals/2014/06/palestinian-prisoners -hunger-strike-israel-kidnapping.html.**

La Presse Canadienne. "Khadir Participe à une Grève de la Faim Symbolique pour Soutenir les Prisonniers Politiques Iraniens." *Le Devoir.* July 25, 2016. **https://www.ledevoir.com/politique /quebec/476272/khadir-participe-a-une -greve-de-la-faim-symbolique-pour-soutenir -les-prisonniers-politiques-iraniens**.

Logan, Joseph. "Up to 20 Die in Police Raids on Turkish Jails." *The Guardian.* December 19, 2000. **https://www.theguardian.com/world/2000 /dec/20/2.**

Margulies, Joseph. *Guantánamo and the Abuse of Presidential Power.* New York: Simon & Schuster. 2007.

Martin, Brian. "Backfire, Repression, and the Theory of Transformative Events." *Mobilization* 11, no. 2 (2006): 249–267.

McFadden, David. "US Military Ending Gitmo Hunger Strike Updates." *Associated Press.* September 23, 2013. **https://www.apnews.com /4b050681b3934368aa61b63dd1cfe523.**

McGreevy, Ronan. "How the Irish Times Reported the Death of Thomas Ashe 100 Years Ago." *Irish Times.* September 25, 2017. **https://www.irishtimes.com/culture/heritage /how-the-irish-times-reported-%20the-death -of-thomas-ashe-100-years-ago-1.3233478.**

Meari, Lena. "*Sumud*: A Palestinian Philosophy of Confrontation in Colonial Prisons." *South Atlantic Quarterly* 113, no. 3 (2014): 547–578.

Metras Global. "Yearning for Freedom." *Instagram.* September 6, 2021. **https://www.instagram.com/p/CTfNVJBtVqb/.**

Michnik, Adam. *Letters from Prison and Other Essays.* Translated by Maya Latynski. Berkeley: University of California Press, 1986.

Miller, Ian. *A History of Force Feeding: Hunger Strikes, Prisons and Medical Ethics, 1909– 1974.* London: Palgrave Macmillan, 2016.

Miller, Ian. "Necessary Torture? Vivisection, Suffragette Force-Feeding, and Responses to Scientific Medicine in Britain c. 1870–1920." *Journal of the History of Medicine and Allied Sciences* 64, no. 3 (2009): 333–372.

Moen, Declan. "Irish Political Prisoners and Post Hunger-Strike Resistance to Criminalisation." In *The British Criminology Conference: Selected Proceedings*, vol. 3, edited by George Mair and Roger Tarling. British Society of Criminology, 2000.

Mohammadi, Mahdia. "تسليم اعتصاب غذای برخی از زندانیان نمی شویم/ اجرای کامل مجازات ها [We Will Not Give in to the Hunger Strike of Some Prisoners/Full Implementation of Punishments]." *Mehr News.* August 23, 2017. **https://bit.ly/30ZS8p6.**

Moore-Gilbert, Kylie, and Fariba Adelkhah. "Australian, French Academics Call for Christmas Eve Hunger Strike." *Center for Human Rights in Iran.* December 24, 2019. **https://iranhumanrights.org/2019/12 /imprisoned-french-australian-academics-call -for-christmas-eve-hunger-strike-iran/.**

Nashif, Esmail. *Palestinian Political Prisoners: Identity and Community.* London: Routledge, 2008.

Nashif, Esmail. "Structures of a Revolutionary Pedagogy: Palestinian Political Captives in Israeli Prisons." In *Revolution and Pedagogy: Interdisciplinary and Transnational Perspectives on Educational Foundations*, edited by E. Thomas Ewing, 163–193. New York: Springer, 2005.

New York Times Editorial Board. "Her Crime? Defending Women's Rights in Iran." *New York Times.* March 13, 2019. **https://www.nytimes.com/2019/03/13 /opinion/iran-nasrin-sotoudeh.html.**

Newton, Huey P. *Revolutionary Suicide.* New York: Harcourt, 1973.

Nofal, Aziza. "[The Liberated Etaf Elian]." *Ultra Palestine.* April 18, 2017. **https://ultrapal.ultrasawt.com/-عطاف-المُحرّرة عليان-والفدائي-الذي-قتلها-عشقًا/عزيزة-نوفل/ذاكرة- وطنية.**

Norman, Julie M. *The Palestinian Prisoners Movement: Resistance and Disobedience.* London: Routledge, 2021.

O'Casey, Sean, Fergus O'Connor, and Anna G. Lang. The Sacrifice of Thomas Ashe. Dublin: Fergus O'Connor, 1918.

Osanloo, Arzoo. "Refusing Mercy: Challenging the State's Monopoly on Violence in Iran." In *Policing and Prisons in the Middle East: Formations of Coercion*, edited by Laleh Khalili and Jillian Schwedler. New York: Columbia University Press, 2010.

Ould Slahi, Mohamedou. *Guantánamo Diary: The Fully Restored Text*. New York: Little, Brown, 2017.

Palestinian Prisoners Society [PPSMO]. "Press Release on the Number of Prisoners Between 1948 and 2018." Supplied by Amani Sarahna, media coordinator. 2018.

Pappé, Ilan. *The Ethnic Cleansing of Palestine*. London: Oneworld Publications, 2006a.

Pappé, Ilan. "The 1948 Ethnic Cleansing of Palestine." *Journal of Palestine Studies* 36, no. 1 (2006b): 6–20.

Parsa, Misagh. *Democracy in Iran: Why It Failed and How It Might Succeed*. Cambridge: Harvard University Press, 2016.

Pelleg-Sryck, Tamar. "The Mysteries of Administrative Detention." In *Threat: Palestinian Political Prisoners in Israel*, edited by Abeer Baker and Anat Matar, 123–135. London: Pluto Press, 2011.

Perrin, Jean-Pierre. "Iran: l'Avocate Nasrin Sotoudeh Écrit Depuis sa Prison pour Défendre les Femmes." *Mediapart*. July 26, 2019. **https://www.mediapart.fr/journal /international/260719/iran-l-avocate-nasrin -sotoudeh-ecrit-depuis-sa-prison-pour -defendre-les-femmes**.

Pilkington, Ed. "Guantánamo Hunger Strikers Able to Challenge Force-Feeding, Court Rules." *The Guardian*. February 11, 2014. **https://www.theguardian.com/world/2014 /feb/11/guantanamo-hunger-strikers-force -feeding-ruling**.

Purvis, June. "Suffragette Hunger Strikes, 100 Years On." *The Guardian*. July 6, 2009. **https://www.theguardian.com /commentisfree/libertycentral/2009/jul/06 /suffragette-hunger-strike-protest**.

Qumsiyeh, Mazin B. *Popular Resistance in Palestine: A History of Hope and Empowerment*. London: Pluto Press, 2011.

Qwaider, Rashid. "Empty Intestines." *Modern Discussion Organization*. January 1, 2013. **https://m.ahewar.org/s.asp?aid=340865**.

Rahal, Malika. "Algeria: Nonviolent Resistance Against French Colonialism, 1830–1950s." In *Recovering Nonviolent History: Civil Resistance in Liberation Struggles*, edited by Maciej Bartkowski, 107–124. Boulder: Lynne Rienner Publishers, 2013.

Reprieve. "7 Things You Didn't Know About Guantanamo Bay." *Reprieve*. August 15, 2018. **https://reprieve.org.uk/update/7-facts -guantanmao-bay/**.

Roberts, Adam. "Introduction." in *Civil Resistance and Power Politics: The Experience of Non-violent Action from Gandhi to the Present*, edited by Adam Roberts and Timothy Garton Ash, 1–24. Oxford: Oxford University Press, 2009.

Robinson, Glenn. *Building a Palestinian State: The Incomplete Revolution*. Bloomington: Indiana University Press, 1997.

Roots and Friends of Palestinian Prisoners [ROOTS]. *Ansar III: The Camp of Slow Death*. Washington: ROOTS, 1988.

Rosenthal, Andrew. "Hurray for Guantanamo Bay." *New York Times*. February 2, 2013. **https://takingnote.blogs.nytimes.com /2012/02/09/hurray-for-guantanamo-bay**.

Russell, Sharman A. *Hunger: An Unnatural History*. New York: Basic Books, 2005.

Ryan, Caitlin. *Bodies, Power, and Resistance in the Middle East: Experiences of Subjectification in the Occupied Palestinian Territories*. London: Routledge, 2015.

Saad, Aida. "Palestinian Political Prisoners: Struggle Behind Iron Bars." *Palestine – PLO Information Bulletin*. July 1–15, 1979. **http://www.newjerseysolidarity.net /plobulletin/vol5no12jul1979/aida_saad .shtml.**

Safieh, Afif. "Gene Sharp: Nonviolent Struggle." *Journal of Palestine Studies* 17, no. 1 (1987): 37–55.

Sazegara, Mohsen, and Maria J. Stephan. "Iran's Islamic Revolution and Nonviolent Struggle." In *Civilian Jihad: Nonviolent Struggle, Democratization, and Governance in the Middle East*, edited by Maria J. Stephan, 185–204. New York: Palgrave Macmillan, 2009.

Scanlan, Stephan J., Laurie Cooper Stoll, and Kimberly Lumm. "Starving for Change: The Hunger Strike and Nonviolent Action, 1906–2004." *Research in Social Movements, Conflicts and Change* 28 (2008): 275–323.

Schmitt, Eric. "A Nation Challenged: Captives; A Concession on Turbans Calms Protest in Cuba Camp." *New York Times*. March 2, 2002.

Schock Kurt. "Nonviolent Action and Its Misconceptions: Insights for Social Scientists, *PS: Political Science and Politics* 36, no. 4 (2003): 705–712.

Schock, Kurt. *Unarmed insurrections: People Power Movements in Nondemocracies*. Minneapolis: University of Minnesota Press, 2005.

Scott, James C. *Weapons of the Weak: Everyday Forms of Peasant Resistance*. New Haven: Yale University Press, 1985.

Scott, Shannon. *The Once and Future Bobby Sands: A Critique of the Material Rhetorical Appeal of the 1981 Hunger Strike in Long Kesh Prison*. PhD dissertation. Seattle: University of Washington, 2004.

Setoudeh, Nasrin. "Nasrin Sotoudeh Begins Hunger Strike in Evin Prison." *CHRI*. August 12, 2020. **https://iranhumanrights.org/2020/08/nasrin -sotoudeh-begins-hunger-strike-in-evin-prison/.**

Setoudeh, Nasrin. "'I miss you my dearest': Nasrin Sotoudeh's Letters to Her Children from Prison." *Amnesty International*. May 2, 2019a. **https://www.amnesty.org/en/latest /campaigns/2019/05/nasrin-sotoudeh -letters-to-her-children-from-prison/.**

Setoudeh, Nasron. "*l'Avocate Nasrin Sotoudeh écrit depuis sa prison pour défendre les femmes* [Letter from Mrs. Nasrin Sotoudeh, Iranian Lawyer, Addressed to the Paris Bar...]." April 10, 2019b. **https://www.avocatparis.org/system/files /editos/courrier_madame_nasrin_sotoudeh.pdf.**

Shalhoub-Kevorkian, Nadera. *Security Theology, Surveillance and the Politics of Fear*. Cambridge: Cambridge University Press, 2015.

Sharp, Gene. "Nonviolent Action." In *Encyclopedia of Violence, Peace, and Conflict*, edited by Lester R. Kurtz and Jennifer E. Turpin, 567–574. London: Academic Press, 1999.

Sharp, Gene. *Sharp's Dictionary of Power and Struggle: Language of Civil Resistance in Conflicts*. New York: Oxford University Press, 2012.

Sharp, Gene. *The Politics of Nonviolent Action*. 3 volumes. Boston: Porter Sargent, 1973.

Sharp, Gene. *Waging Nonviolent Struggle: 20th Century Practice and 21st Century Potential*. Boston: Extending Horizons, 2005.

Shawahna, Ali. *Al Karama Hunger Strike 2012: Extensive Study of the Details of the Strike from Preparation to Victory*. Gaza: Mohjat al-Quds, 2013.

Sherwood, Harriet. "Palestinian Prisoners End Hunger Strike." *The Guardian.* May 14, 2012. **https://www.theguardian.com/world/2012 /may/14/palestinian-prisoners-end-hunger -strike**.

Shwaikh, Malaka. "Dynamics of Prison Resistance: Hunger Strikes by Palestinian Political Prisoners in Israeli Prisons." *Jerusalem Quarterly* no. 75 (Autumn 2018): 78–90.

Shwaikh, Malaka. "Engendering Hunger Strikes: Palestinian Women in Israeli Prisons." *British Journal of Middle Eastern Studies* 49, no. 4 (2020): 507–525.

Shwaikh, Malaka. "What the Galboa Prison Break Symbolises for Palestinians." *TRT World*. September 7, 2021. **https://www.trtworld.com/opinion/what -the-galboa-prison-break-symbolises-for -palestinians-49772**.

[Shwaikh], Malaka Mohammed. "'I Will Not Withdraw from the Battle for Freedom': The Story of Samer Issawi." *Samidoun: Palestinian Prisoner Solidarity Network*. 01 January 2013. **https://samidoun.net/2013/01/story-of-samer -issawi/**.

Simanowitz, Stephan. "Rapper's Hunger Strike Shows Power of Ancient Form of Protest." *Huffington Post*. October 22, 2016. **https://bit.ly/2tcY6kb**.

Stephan, Maria J. *Civilian Jihad: Nonviolent Struggle, Democratization, and Governance in the Middle East*. New York: Palgrave Macmillan, 2009.

Stephan, Maria J., and Erica Chenoweth. "Why Civil Resistance Works: The Strategic Logic of Nonviolent Conflict." *International Security* 33, no. 1 (2008): 7–44.

Sumina, Svetlana, and Steven Gilmore. "The Failure of International Law in Palestine." *The Scholar: St. Mary's Law Review on Race and Social Justice* 20, no. 2 (2018): 135–188.

Taraki, Lisa. "[Development of Political Awareness in the Occupied Territories Before the Intifada, 1967–1987]." *Afaq Falastiniya* no. 5 (1990): 27–58.

Thompson, Heather Ann. *Blood in the Water: The Attica Prison Uprising of 1971 and Its Legacy*. New York: Pantheon Books, 2016.

Thoreau, Henry David. "Civil Disobedience." *A Yankee in Canada with Anti-Slavery and Reform Papers*. Boston: Ticknor and Fields, 1866.

Tisdall, Simon. "Freed Iranian Rights Lawyer: 'I've a Bad Feeling About the Women I Left Behind." *The Guardian*. June 1, 2014.

Touma, Wasileh, in al-Amital, Muna. "Wasileh Touma: The Story of 28 Years of Waiting for a Dream to Come True." *BNFSJ*. May 24, 2021. **https://bnfsj.net/post/94/-٨٢-وسيلة-طعمة-حكاية عام-ا-من-الانتظار-لتحقيق-الحلم.**

United Nations Human Rights Office of the High Commissioner's Human Rights in Cooperation with the International Bar Association. *Human Rights in the Administration of Justice: A Manual on Human Rights for Judges, Prosecutors and Lawyers*. New York: United Nations, 2003.

United Nations Office for the Coordination of Humanitarian Affairs [UN OCHA]. "Over 700 Road Obstacles Control Palestinian Movement Within the West Bank." *Monthly Humanitarian Bulletin*. October 8, 2018. **https://www.ochaopt.org/content/over -700-road-obstacles-control-palestinian -movement-within-west-bank.**

Veracini, Lorenzo. "The Other Shift: Settler Colonialism, Israel, and the Occupation." *Journal of Palestine Studies* 42, no. 2 (2013): 26–42.

Wilson, Elizabeth. "'People Power' and the Problem of Sovereignty in International Law." *Duke Journal of Comparative & International Law* 26 (2016): 581–586.

Wilson, Elizabeth. *People Power Movements and International Human Rights: Creating a Legal Framework.* Washington: ICNC Press, 2017.

Wink, Walter. *Violence and Nonviolence in South Africa: Jesus' Third Way.* Philadelphia: New Society Publishers, 1987.

Wintour, Patrick. "Zaghari-Ratcliffe to Go on Hunger Strike for Fellow Detainee in Iran." *The Guardian.* December 29, 2019. **https://www.theguardian.com/news/2019 /dec/29/zaghari-ratcliffe-to-go-on-hunger -strike-for-fellow-detainee-in-iran.**

World Medical Association [WMA]. *WMA Declaration of Tokyo.* September 6, 2022.

Institute for Crime and Justice Policy Research. *World Prison Brief: Iran.* 2019. **http://www.prisonstudies.org/country/iran.**

Wren, Christopher. "Terrorist or Freedom Fighter? Pretoria Debates Whom to Amnesty." *New York Times.* June 3, 1990. **https://www.nytimes.com/1990/06/03/world /terrorist-or-freedom-fighter-pretoria-debates -whom-to-amnesty.html.**

Younis, Mohammed. "Hamas, on Fatah's Path, Investing in Popular Resistance." *Al Hayat.* 2018.

Zamani, Shahrokh. "نوشته‌های شاهرخ زمانی از زندان Nivishtahayi Shahrokh Zamani az zindan [The Prison Writings of Shahrokh Zamani]." Workers' Action Committee. 2015. **https://www.marxists.org/archive/zamani /works/jail-statement.htm.**

Ziadah, Rafeef. "The Palestine I Know." *We Teach Life.* 2016. **https://www.musixmatch.com/lyrics/Rafeef -Ziadah/The-Palestine-I-Know.**

Acknowledgments

Malaka would like to first thank her family (her parents Najah and Mohammed, siblings, nephews, and nieces) whose support throughout this research has been constantly unwavering. This work would not have been possible without the generous support of a community of ex-prisoners, ex-hunger strikers, their families, and supportive communities from Palestine to Jordan, Northern Ireland, South Africa, England and Wales, Tunisia, and Qatar. I am also grateful for friends and colleagues whose care and support help me grow: Sara Abbas, Hasnaa Mokhtar, Jasmine Gani, Roxani Krystalli, Jaremey McMullin, Ashjan Ajour, and Candance Amani—thank you for being generous with your time and insights.

Rebecca would like to thank her family (Beth, Kate, and Brenda Gould) as well as the many generous people who provided insight and critiques with respect to matters relating to Palestine. Seth Anziska, Mohammad El-Khatib, Bilal Hamamra, Tariq Modood, Yana Shabana, and Yair Wallach have been particularly generous with their time and thoughts. Kayvan as always was a priceless source of knowledge and insight for all matters connected to Iran.

We both would like to thank all groups and individuals in Palestine and elsewhere that centre the voices of prisoners, provide them with legal support, and advocate for their rights.

Finally, we are particularly grateful to ICNC for including this volume in their series and to Bruce Pearson, Steve Chase, and Maciej Bartkowski for their meticulous edits and generous support in the process of writing our monograph.

About the Authors

Malaka Mohammed Shwaikh is a Palestinian academic from the Gaza Strip, based at the University of St. Andrews in Scotland where she teaches and researches prisons as spaces of power, resistance, and peacebuilding. She is the author of several works at the intersection of prison resistance and power, including "Dynamics of Prison Resistance: Hunger Strikes by Palestinian Political Prisoners in Israeli Prisons" (*Jerusalem Quarterly,* 2018), "Engendering Hunger Strikes: Palestinian Women in Israeli Prisons" (*British Journal of Middle Eastern Studies,* 2020), and most recently, "Prison Periods: Bodily Resistance to Gendered Control" (*Journal of Feminist Scholarship,* 2022). She finds purpose and joy in giving back to the community and being involved in social justice work. Her most recent and ongoing project (since 2021) is Freelancers in Gaza, with Candace Amani, to connect freelancers in Gaza with clients around the world and provide them with tailored mentorship.

Rebecca Ruth Gould is the author of numerous works at the intersection of aesthetics and politics, including *Writers and Rebels: The Literature of Insurgency in the Caucasus* (Yale University Press, 2016), *The Persian Prison Poem: Sovereignty and the Political Imagination* (Edinburgh University Press, 2021), and, most recently, *Erasing Palestine: Free Speech and Palestinian Freedom* (Verso Books, 2023). Together with Malaka Shwaikh, she is the author of "The Palestine Exception to Academic Freedom: Intertwined Stories from the Frontlines of UK-Based Palestine Activism," *Biography: An Interdisciplinary Quarterly* (2020), which brought together their shared interests relating to Palestinian liberation. She is Professor, Islamic World & Comparative Literature, at the University of Birmingham, where she directs the GlobalLIT project.